The Rolling Stones

Turner Publishing, Inc.
ATLANTA

The Rolling Stones:
black and white blues, 1963

Photographs by Gus Coral

Text by David Hinckley
and Debra Rodman

Published by Turner Publishing, Inc.
A Subsidiary of Turner Broadcasting System, Inc.
1050 Techwood Drive, N.W.
Atlanta, Georgia 30318

Library of Congress Cataloging-in-Publication Data

Coral, Gus.
The Rolling Stones: black and white blues, 1963/
photographs by Gus Coral; text by David Hinckley
and Debra Rodman. —1st ed.
p.   cm.

ISBN 1-57036-150-9

1. Rolling Stones. 2. Rolling Stones—Pictorial
works. 3. Rock musicians—England—Pictorial works.
4. Rock music—England—1961—1970—Pictorial works.
I. Hinckley, David. II. Rodman, Debra. III. Title.

ML421.R64C67 1995

782.42166'092'2—dc20

[B]   94-37539
                                             CIP
                                             MN

Distributed in the U.S. by: Distributed in the U.K. by:
Andrews and McMeel   Pegasus Sales and Dist. Ltd.
A Universal Press Syndicate Co.   Unit 5B, Causeway Park
4900 Main Street   Wilderspool Causeway
Kansas City, Missouri 64112   Warrington, Cheshire WA4 6QE

First Edition 10 9 8 7 6 5 4 3 2 1

Printed in the U.S.A.   Film by Capitol Engraving Co.,
                                   Nashville, Tennessee

                                   Printed by McQuiddy Printing Co.,
                                   Nashville, Tennessee

Kevin Mulroy- EDITOR
Katherine Buttler- EDITORIAL
Elaine Streithof- ART DIRECTOR
Christine Holmes- PRODUCTION MANAGER

For
Luke

"They were

down.

They had
problems.

I remember

I told
them if
they

abandon

what they

had going

in the
band,

they were

stupid."

—BO DIDDLEY

Who Do You Love?

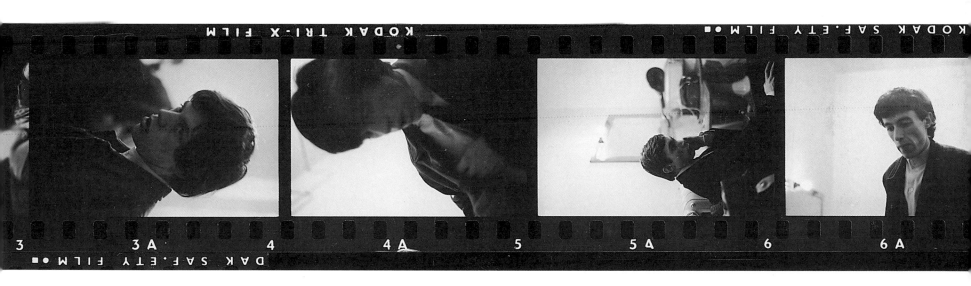

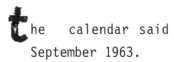

the calendar said
September 1963.

But calendars don't always tell the whole truth and for the Rolling Stones, five cocky kids who were turning rhythm and blues into rock 'n' roll in a way no one else had done before, September 1963 was the night before Christmas.

They just didn't know it yet.

What they knew was that they had landed a tour of Northern England with three of their rock 'n' roll idols, Bo Diddley, Little Richard, and the Everly Brothers, and that their first single release, a version of Chuck Berry's "Come On" which they despised, had performed well enough for them to be asked, pressured even, to produce a second. Beyond offering a chance for musical atonement, this was obviously a favorable career indicator.

Still, what they physically held in hand—the modest payday from a package tour of one-nighters and the chance to throw one more 45-rpm record into the vast cavern of popular music—left them well below any threshold of the success toward which they had been maniacally pushing since the band came together earlier that year. Their greater encouragement at this point had to come from the sheer instinct, the embryonic sense that teenage ears perked up and teenage hormones crashed into overdrive when the Rolling Stones delivered their high-voltage hybrid of blues, rhythm and blues, and rock 'n' roll. Before the Stones had played a note outside the tiny clubs of London, their fan club had three hundred members who would, at the mere mention of the fact a band

member favored yellow socks, mail in sackfuls of them.

These tours are the kinds of packages an entertainer likes to see under the tree, and looking back, it hardly seems surprising that for the Rolling Stones the bright wrappings soon fell away to reveal glass slippers.

But in September 1963, they could just as easily have revealed covered lumps of coal, and that's what these pictures and this book are about: the Rolling Stones at a time which now may seem either mythic or simply very long ago, in the final hours before they knew whether playing music would ever advance beyond personal pleasure to a means of earning a living.

In 1963, when young British and American boys were beginning to form rock bands as casually as they combed their hair, hundreds of tours resembled the one that took the Stones on a 36-night stand through Northern England: a line-up of artists who, though not quite stars, had either enough future or enough past so their arrival in a slightly out-of-the-way town would constitute an event, or at least a night for which the locals would part with a pound or so.

The starting date of the tour, September 29, 1963, fell one month and one day after Martin Luther King Jr. gave his "I Have a Dream" speech in Washington, D.C. It's unlikely any of the Stones—Mick Jagger, vocals; Brian Jones, guitar and harmonica; Keith Richards, rhythm guitar; Bill Wyman, bass; and Charlie Watts, drums—paid it much mind, their

▶

Brian Jones burned to sing. Keith Richards, before he was ten, had soloed with a boys choir at Westminster Abbey. But one of the few points on which no one ever argued was who would front the Rolling Stones— Mick Jagger.

interest in America being limited primarily to news of music, and for the most part, not even current music. Certainly no Stone had a clue that before the decade was over, they would be playing torrential rock 'n' roll to stadiums filled with thousands of fans or that their music and attitudes would in some minds represent the flip side of King's dream—a journey into the darkness where Dr. King had summoned the light.

On this date the Rolling Stones' dream was far more modest, though no less burning. If they nailed this tour, if they came back bigger than when they left, if the following they had built in the blues clubs of London was not just a core of cultists, it would tell them they had a real shot at making a living by playing their wild new music—music of their own, music foreign to their parents, though in the end not nearly as adversarial as the new generation hoped and the old generation feared.

"We thought this music was absolutely new," says Keith Richards today, shaking his head and grinning. "That's how we felt about it. It was only after we'd been around a few more years that we realized this had been going on forever. Mozart rocks, man!"

Still, reassuring truths from the long lens of history rarely have a soothing effect on those whose music is being supplanted, particularly when the agents of change seem to be challenging not only the sound of mainstream popular music, but its look and its attitude. Today, Mick Jagger in his wrinkled shirt and Keith Richards with the slung-back guitar look

There may have been some point in Keith Richards' life at which he lacked confidence that things would somehow work out with his music. Or, then again, there may have been no such point at all.

incredibly young. In 1963, to the popular music establishment, Mick looked like a smirking nightmare from music's dark unwashed underside and Keith like the cocksure new gunslinger who might as well have ambled in with a Gatling gun as a Harmony guitar.

This prospect of imminent change in the cultural guard offered a particularly strong adrenalin rush in early-'60s Britain, a country only beginning to feel it had put its life back together after the physical and psychological devastation of World War II.

Less than six months later, it would become apparent that this new music, a simple British adaptation of American rock 'n' roll, had become a careening train, and that catching a forward car could literally open up the world for a band like the Rolling Stones. But on September 29, no one knew the scope of the horizon. No one knew if rock 'n' roll was going to crash and burn on the next curve, as grownups were still comfortably predicting. And even if it didn't, the Rolling Stones themselves had no idea whether their own music—a home-brewed gumbo of Muddy Waters, Bo Diddley, Chuck Berry, and Buddy Holly, built on a jazz-rooted rhythm section and interlocking guitars—held anywhere near the potential appeal of the pop/rock already bringing fame and fortune to their friends from Liverpool, the Beatles.

Fortunately for the Stones, they could have gotten no stronger reassurance and no better jumpstart than this tour, on which they were originally signed to open for a pair of American headliners, the Everly

Brothers and Bo Diddley. Various other British acts shared the warm-up spot, including pop-ballad singer Julie Grant and a saxophone combo called the Flintstones. After the first half-dozen shows, with mixed box-office results, Little Richard was flown in to provide another headline name.

Tour promoter Don Arden, like all concert promoters of the era, had begun his career in the pop/vaudeville/variety show days and would not have minded a bit had vaudeville sprung back to life. It was so ordered, so reliable. In its absence, rock 'n' roll had become the siren of the young at what struck most promoters as a somewhat unsettling cost. This ranged from the breakdown of traditional stage decorum to the perception that rock 'n' roll and its artists were so ephemeral that anyone booking an act three months in advance could wind up on show night with a box-office corpse.

There were also few native British rock 'n' roll stars, and since popular music has always thrived in direct proportion to the light cast by stars at the top, promoters in 1963 were concerned that this semi-infant was crawling along without so much as an Elvis Presley to illuminate the way. Clean-cut Cliff Richard, the biggest British name of the moment, was a knock-off, an ersatz second-generation Elvis who could give you the moves without seeming to quite understand why they worked the first time.

Arden's plan, then, was rooted in conventional promoter wisdom. He would bring over a couple of big

names from America, a few years removed from their commercial prime so they'd work for less, and package them with a fistful of lesser-known British acts who, with enough local following to sell tickets, would also be so grateful for a place on this relatively high-profile show that they would work for next to nothing.

As faithfully recorded by Wyman, a methodical and rather serious chap who took on the role of scribe and historian before anyone knew there would be more than a footnote to write, the Stones were paid twenty-one pounds, five shillings per show, or about $100 before expenses.

What Arden was not envisioning is what we now see in the rearview mirror: a flashpoint at which two major modern popular musical forces intersected in person before diverging again, only this time with the student pulling in front of the teacher. Bo Diddley, the Everly Brothers, and Little Richard formed a nice representative cross-section of the American pioneers who had laid down the road for rock 'n' roll—the road on which attentive British students like the Stones would soon roll to glory.

Not that Arden cared much about carving himself a place in history. He was doing this tour for his pocketbook, and if that sounds unromantic, the truth is that so, pretty much, were the others.

Bo Diddley, Little Richard, and the Everly Brothers had all been on the road for a decade or more by 1963. Since this was many years before early rockers had established a semi-comfortable circuit where they could play to nostalgic middle-aged fans, they were all undergoing the frustration of watching their marketability fade as the next generation picked up their moves. Fifties rockers were still in demand around America by 1963, but not so much that a guaranteed month of work overseas didn't look good. Bo Diddley's face tells the story: one more bare-bulb dressing room, one more paper-plate dinner, one more payday.

For the Stones, whose popularity in those tiny blues clubs of London had provided the first indication that they could disprove everything their parents said and never have to get a "real" job, the tour would take them out of London for the first time—Richards had never been north of London. It offered an opportunity for them to broaden their audience, play bigger venues, get their name on the bill with some of their idols, and at the very least have an adventure. "It was a period of anticipation, of barriers being crossed and dreams being realized," Wyman wrote in his autobiography, *Stone Alone*.

He also added, not incidentally, that the awakenings turned out to be sexual as well as geographic. Enough willing female fans waited at each stop that Wyman noted in his diary the "uncharacteristic" night in Newcastle when hotel security wouldn't let the band members bring guests to their rooms "and we had to go to bed alone." Ordinarily, he adds, the road was particularly fertile turf for him, since back home he was married.

No one
knew
if

rock 'n'

roll

was going to

crash

and

burn

on the

next

curve.

Still, pleasant as it must have seemed for the Stones to relax after a show with no deeper concern than "the blonde or the brunette or both," a larger issue did linger in the air: whether these five musicians would continue to play together as a band.

If that question seems like foolish melodrama with thirty years of hindsight, ask anyone who has ever plucked, pounded, or sung a note in a band and they will confirm that at this stage, before the real signs of professional success like money or records or major media deals have come in, breakup is always an open option. If a better idea or more promising band had come along, any Stone could have rolled out the door. After all, that's how they came to be Rolling Stones in the first place, because their previous bands hadn't been going far enough fast enough.

The roots of the intra-band tension centered, as it frequently would for the next several years, on Brian Jones, whose musical fluency was matched by his personal instability. "The most brilliant musician I ever knew," Richards calls him, and not only for the blur of his fingers on a guitar. "He could pick up any instrument and in ten minutes he could play it. Give me a saxophone and I couldn't even tell you which end to blow in."

Riding in large part on his superior musicianship, Jones had assumed the leadership of the early Stones. He booked the dates; he called the rehearsals. It's a function assumed by one member of virtually every young band.

Jagger and Richards, however, were not born to follow, and it soon became clear that wielding power in the Stones required political as well as musical skills—specifically, the ability to forge a coalition with at least one of the other major players. This initially led to a series of shifting alliances, including Mick and Brian vs. Keith, and Keith and Brian vs. Mick, but by late 1963 several factors had combined to leave Jones increasingly the odd Stone out.

For one thing, the Stones' new manager, Andrew Loog Oldham, had begun pushing the band to write their own songs, for both creative and financial reasons. While Keith and Mick willingly took on the challenge, this proved an aspect of music at which Brian showed little proficiency—nor would he accept a collaborative role.

"It was impossible to write a song with Brian," says Richards, "because he insisted on controlling everything." This would have been fine if he were writing great songs, but that seems not to have been the case. Linda Lawrence, who as Brian's current girlfriend landed herself a job as hairdresser on the 1963 tour, says, "He was always writing songs, but he was very insecure about them. He wrote songs by himself, for himself."

Brian's long-term leadership was further weakened when it was discovered, halfway through the tour, that he was secretly paying himself five pounds a week more than the other band members. Wyman quotes pianist, chief roadie, and lifelong sixth Stone

▶

Brian played any instrument he could get his hands on—harmonica, saxophone, sitar, whatever. But he seemed to find the most possibilities in the guitar, because that's the one to which he returned most regularly.

Ian Stewart as pronouncing a simple and final judgment: "That was it from then on. It was over for him as leader."

Rather than seek reconciliation, however, recalls Linda Lawrence, Brian inadvertently compounded the estrangement: "Brian wanted to sing very badly, and for a while on the tour, he and Mick traded off the lead for a few songs. By the end of the tour, the competition between him and Mick began. It manifested itself in little things, like Brian wanting to know who had more fan mail. Then when they started to take speed to stay awake, I began seeing the paranoia that Brian became famous for and he lost his confidence. . . . "

Ironically, it was only a few months earlier that Richards says he and Brian had kicked around the possibility of breaking off into a duet act with twin guitars, like the Everly Brothers. One reason the idea died was Richards' realization that he and Brian could never compose any original songs for their act.

Whatever deep-rooted or temporal forces threatened the survival of these early Stones, Bo Diddley says they talked with him during the northern tour about splitting. He advised them not to: "They were fixin' to break up, but I told them to hang in there. They were down. They had problems in the band. I remember I told them, if they abandon what they had going in the band, they were stupid."

In any case, it's unlikely any Stone would have left before the end of this tour, where every night

presented a free master seminar in stage performance. "I could have sat in the wings forever watching," Wyman later wrote. "We learned something new every night."

Nor, for all the Stones' love of black music, did they neglect the cool harmonies and gentle rippling guitars of Don and Phil Everly. "Everything we did then, the weaving two guitars together until they became indistinguishable, was us trying to be the Everly Brothers," says Keith Richards.

From Little Richard, they learned the art of a rock 'n' roll show as one prolonged explosion of manic foreplay. "When the lights went down, before he even came on stage," Richards recalls, "he'd let the band riff on 'Lucille' for five, ten minutes. By then the audience was going crazy, and finally he'd come out at the back, or one of the sides. The spotlight would hit him and the place was one solid roar."

"My ideal show," says Mick Jagger, "is an hour of high-energy, straight rock 'n' roll. No ballads."

They studied the hypnotic guitar and equally hypnotic hips of Bo Diddley. Eight years earlier, Elvis Presley had studied that same bump-and-grind when Bo was playing Harlem's Apollo Theater, and a few months later, Elvis slipped some of Bo's moves into his apocalyptic January 1956 performance on *The Ed Sullivan Show*. Most of America assumed they were all his own.

The Stones' opening-night set September 29, at the New Victoria Theater in London, was a ten-

▶

Put a tie and jacket on most people and they stiffen up and act right. Put a tie and jacket on Little Richard and watch him become a howling maniac.

minute sprint through four late-'50s R&B songs: the Coasters' "Poison Ivy," "Fortune Teller," "Come On," and Barrett Strong's "Money." Ordinarily they did at least one Bo Diddley song in any performance, but Brian Jones told the press they would not do any on this tour, as a gesture of respect for the master's presence. To underscore this with something tangible, Mick, Brian, and Keith gave Bo a set of gold cufflinks.

Even without Diddley's "Mona" or "Cracking Up," the Stones' performance grew so strong as weeks passed that on the closing night of the tour, November 3 back in London's Odeon Theater, fans were chanting "We want the Stones!" and throwing paper cups at the Everlys for having the nerve to close the show instead of letting the Stones play all night so they could keep dancing in the aisles.

Chagrined that fans would treat the pioneers so shabbily, the Stones considered this disrespect little less than an act of defilement. But they were hardly upset to be sending out their own sparks, and the loud approval they heard at many stops on this tour signaled that word had indeed spread beyond London. In fact, that buzz led to the pictures in this book, which represent the first extended photographic look of its type at the pre-fame Stones.

The tour had barely begun when Dick Fontaine heard enough intriguing rumbles that he decided he would size up these Rolling Stones on Sunday, October 6, at the Capitol Theater in Cardiff, Wales. Fontaine, who produced a program on Britain's

northwest region for Granada Television, was always scouting for hot new trends—a year earlier, he was the first TV director to film the Beatles at the Cavern Club. Thinking he might be able to feature the Stones in the pop music segment of his show, he hired freelance photographer Gus Coral to take a series of informal stills which would help him decide how they might best be presented by a television camera.

So Fontaine and Coral showed up backstage at the Capitol that night and were told the band was next door at the area's only open cafe, prepping for the first of the night's two shows. This was standard procedure: The artists arrived in town, set up their equipment, and did a primitive soundcheck, then killed time until the show started. Depending on the distance from London, they might drive their van back home when the second show ended, or they might pile into a modestly priced hotel which, with any luck, had no policy against opposite-sex visitors.

On this particular evening, Coral found the Stones sitting at a couple of booths complaining about the houndstooth jackets they had been directed to wear on stage by their booking agent, a thirty-five-year-old traditionalist named Eric Easton.

Like Brian Epstein with the Beatles, Easton felt a performing group should not risk alienating anyone with its attire. The Stones felt the criterion should be whether the attire alienated the band, and by Cardiff they were on the brink of abandoning the houndstooth, feeling it did not represent their music or atti-

From
Little
Richard,
they
learned
the
art
of a
rock 'n'
roll show
as one
prolonged
explosion
of
manic
foreplay.

tude. As these pictures attest, the uprising had reached the point where the upfront players shed the jackets after a song or two—though Charlie Watts stuck it out.

While this sounds like minor stuff by the standards of subsequent rock-star rebellion, it was at the time an act of authentic revolution. Decades of tradition dictated that performers dress up, and even today, road veterans of the '40s, '50s, and '60s talk about the passing of stage uniforms the way Coke drinkers talk about the demise of 6 $1/2$-ounce green bottles: From that moment on, everything was a little less classy and never quite as good. "When you're there to give a show, and people are paying good money to see it," says 1950s R&B legend Ruth Brown, "looking your best is one of the ways you show them respect. You come out in ripped bluejeans, what are you saying about what you think of them? When you're on stage, you should be the best-dressed person in the house."

It might seem mildly ironic, given the way he stuck with the houndstooth in Cardiff, that Watts is credited in Stones lore as the first to discover one night that his houndstooth was nowhere to be found. Sorry, mate, love to wear it, but it's mysteriously missing. In truth, even though Brian was known in the band as Mr. Shampoo—a title Coral's photos show to be well earned—Charlie has always been the most fastidious about his wardrobe. In the notorious 1966 group-drag photo for the "Have You Seen Your Mother Baby" picture sleeve, the other four compete fervently to achieve the highest camp while Charlie stands to the side looking quite ready to go out on the town.

Back in Cardiff, meanwhile, Gus Coral followed the Stones to the theater and photographed everyone as they prepped for the show. This wasn't difficult, since the common dressing room was a tiny cubicle without a door. Coral's biggest challenge was the sheer number of bodies: The Stones were sharing the room with the Everlys, Little Richard, Bo Diddley, Bo's maraca player Jerome Green, and Bo's half sister The Duchess. Not to mention Linda Lawrence, odd stagehands, and a few fans seen here dropping in on Little Richard, the only one of the American acts with a long-standing reputation in the British Isles.

By night's end, Coral had taken some 150 pictures, and the Stones asked if he would be interested in photographing them the next day in London, where they were using the tour's weekly Monday off to squeeze in a recording session at Holborn's De Lane Lea Studios.

There was a certain urgency here, because they needed a new single and they needed it fast. "Come On" wasn't an awful record, but it was a first record, and the Stones knew it: a feel-your-way-into-it tryout with a too-fast tempo which made them no great number of new fans and was by now mostly embarrassing to band members, who frequently refused to play it live. Unloved and unpromoted, "Come On" was history and the Stones were eager to show they could do better.

But while the Stones were already a first-rate live band and getting better all the time, translating that talent into the creation of hit records under studio conditions would be quite different. For one thing, an R&B or rock classic that can be whipped into a powerful piece of work on stage can easily come out on record as one more remake, one more imitation rendered instantly superfluous by the mere existence of the original.

"You don't see a lot of Buddy Holly and Jerry Lee Lewis records being remade," says Richards. "And to me that's the highest compliment—that you did it so well you made it your own and no one else can match it."

This was a standard the Stones themselves would later attain frequently, to Richards' satisfaction, but in mid-1963 they didn't have that option. They had no songs of their own, and unlike their American counterparts, British artists did not even have a Brill Building to which they could turn for a dozen submissions. Not that it would have helped much. The Brill Building was not set up to serve a band; it was designed for singers with backup musicians, and not in their most fractious moments did the Stones consider any member of the band to be a backup musician.

Keith has never been known as a guitar virtuoso along the lines of an Eric Clapton. To this day, it's often unclear whether he's playing lead or rhythm guitar. These are facts in which he takes considerable satisfaction.

Coral first found the group together in a café before the Capitol show—Brian voicing displeasure with their houndstooth "uniforms." Ironically, Charlie Watts, who wore his jacket faithfully, was the first of the Stones to permanently misplace it. . . .

▶

Mick and Keith would call Brian "Mr. Shampoo," after the times he would use all the hot water in the Edith Grove flat to ensure his blond locks remained flaxen. And purely on those terms, he was right; he had the best hair in the band.

▶

When you come right down to it, the Stones were right: The houndstooth jackets did look ridiculous. But then, John Lennon looked ridiculous singing "Twist and Shout" in a Beatlesuit, too.

Jerome Green played maracas for Bo Diddley, which isn't a bad bit of inspiration when you consider Diddley's beat. Green was also a talented sideman back in Chicago.

Recording studios always look like the kind of room your mother used to tell you to clean up, which may be one reason rock 'n' roll musicians find them irresistible.

◄

Backstage in the dressing
room, in between shows
at the Capitol Theater,
Mick keeps the energy
level high.

◄

Bill Wyman, several years
older than the other band
members, shaved five
of those years off for
press purposes so no one
would think he was an old
guy trying to infiltrate
rock 'n' roll. The irony is,
he kind of looked like
an old guy anyway.

▶

Brian Jones was the Stone who could pick up any instrument and give it a voice within ten minutes. For a band whose Holy Grail was rhythm and blues out of the Mississippi delta by way of Chicago, no instrument except the guitar was more valuable than the blues harp.

▶

The rule for dressing rooms on the circuit where the Stones started was that the lights should work and the mirror should be big enough so you could see your jacket and your hair at the same time.

Mick Jagger today will tell you he still quite likes the format of those early shows—a machine-gun burst of rock 'n' roll, song-song-song-song, then out.

For a British Isles rock 'n' roll fan, an audience with Little Richard was like an American poetry fan meeting, say, the Irish poet W. B. Yeats.

Real footlights,
reflecting brightly off
their white shirts with
the billowing long sleeves.
A glittering curtain,
reflecting those footlights
back. The big time.

While Mick was the
vocalist, Brian was almost
a co-frontman, teasing the
crowd with his harmonica,
guitar, and nice clean hair.

page 33.

"Jazz and

Classical.

That's what
I remember

from the

BBC

in the

fifties.

That's what

you

grew up

hearing."

—KEITH RICHARDS

All I Have to Do Is Dream

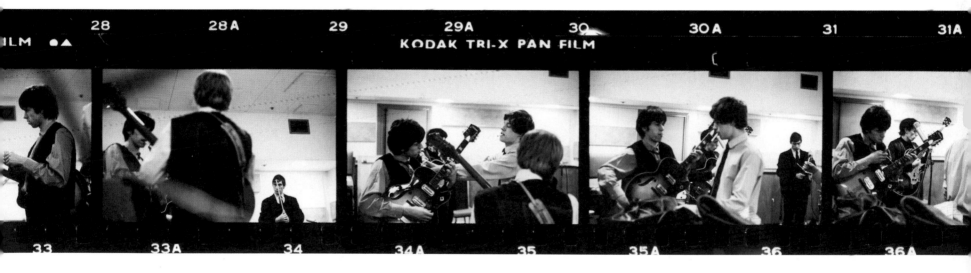

So Andrew Loog Oldham
spent several weeks

in the summer of '63 dipping into the good old American R&B well, and he finally found a tune he felt was neither too obscure nor too overdone: the Coasters' "Poison Ivy." Written by the sturdy American team of Jerry Leiber and Mike Stoller, it required Mick to sing about needing "an ocean of Calamine lotion," but it had some growl, too, and the Stones dutifully went to Decca Records' studio to record it.

The Stones had been signed by Decca earlier in 1963, largely because Decca's A&R (Artist & Repertoire) man, Dick Rowe, had a monkey on his back the size of King Kong. In 1962 he had turned down the Beatles, and he knew that only a signing of similar magnitude would prevent him from wearing that designation like a neon tattoo for the remainder of his professional life.

Consequently, Rowe needed the Stones' second record as much as the band did, and when they arrived for the "Poison Ivy" session, he had Decca producer Michael Barclay on hand to guide matters along. It was an unfortunate match: "The Stones thought he was a fuddy-duddy," Rowe later told writer Philip Norman, "and he thought they were mad."

The session finally yielded a useable take which was assigned a release number, but at the last moment both sides realized they didn't need another single that no one liked, and it was scrapped, along with the projected B-side, "Fortune Teller." Both

▶

For all their reputation as rumpled tomcats, the Stones included three guys who cared a lot about how they looked: Mick, Brian, and Charlie. Keith was somewhat more sartorially challenged, but still managed a shirt and tie in the recording studio.

would eventually surface as more or less throwaways on a 1964 "Saturday Club" compilation album.

So Oldham, searching for a better way to capture on vinyl the power he knew the Stones could produce on stage, brought them to the De Lane Lea Studios on September 14 and 15 and told them to play as if they were in front of a live audience. They had the freedom to do this independent production because Oldham had shrewdly insisted on a contract wherein the Stones could make their own recordings and lease them to Decca—a goldmine if they became successful, since they, rather than the company, would own the masters. This brilliant ploy had been suggested to Oldham by his mentor, Phil Spector.

Musically, the switch to a non-Decca setting worked well enough to produce the Stones' first studio classic: a chilling rendition of Arthur Alexander's "You Better Move On," where Mick's measured vocal builds beautifully over Brian's and Keith's acoustic guitars.

Unfortunately, "You Better Move On" proved to be a long-term classic rather than an instant radio-hit, and while they also cut better-than-acceptable renditions of Chuck Berry's "Bye Bye Johnny" and Barrett Strong's "Money" over those two days, none was felt to have the proper punch for a single. As the northern tour approached, then, committing the Stones to six weeks on the road, Oldham became increasingly concerned about that second single. He had already initiated what he hoped would be the long-term

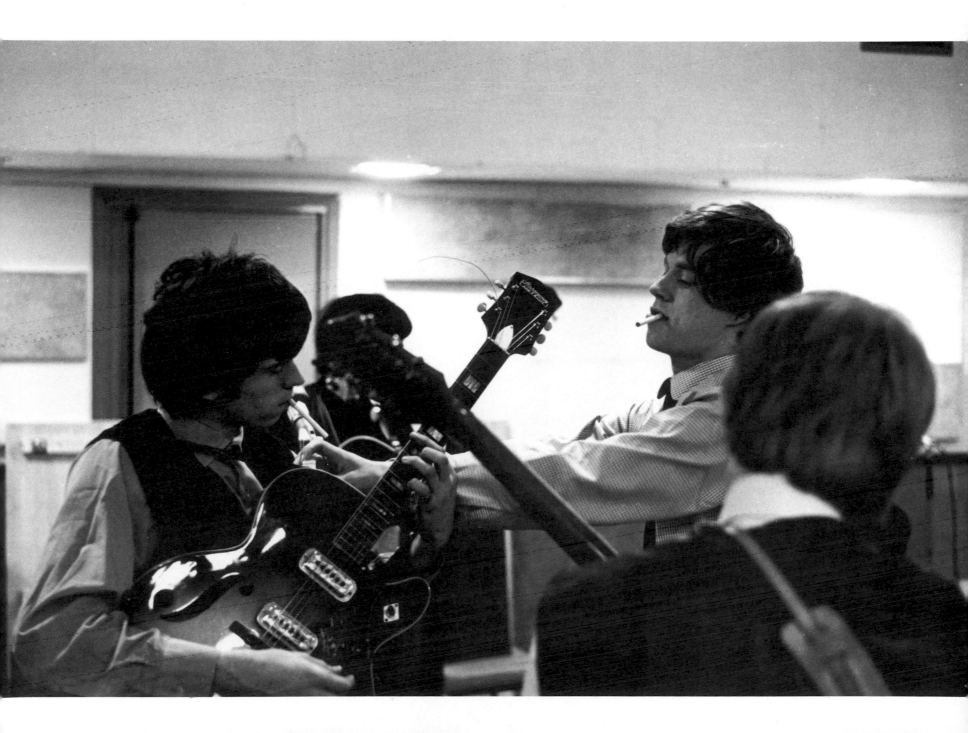

solution, driving Mick and Keith to write songs of their own, but at this point they were closer to Spinal Tap than Lennon-McCartney.

"The story about Andrew locking me and Mick in the kitchen is absolutely true," Richards says. "He told us we couldn't come out until we had a song. So Mick and I sat there staring at the tape recorder, thinking, 'What do we know about writing songs?' We'd go to the fridge, where there was maybe half a week-old sandwich. We smoked. And after a while we realized he was serious, he really wasn't going to let us out, so we had better at least try to come up with something.

"By then, if nothing else, we really had to pee. So we finally put something together, and banged on the door. Andrew got up from watching television or whatever he was doing and we gave him the tape recorder and headed for the bathroom."

Richards says that first song was "As Tears Go By," which was recorded a year or so later by Jagger's then-girlfriend Marianne Faithfull and became enough of a hit so the Stones later released their own version. It's not a terribly sophisticated piece of music, with its simple melody. But while Richards doesn't care for it, it's hardly a tune without charm.

In any case, learning to write music requires much the same process as learning to play or sing it, and for Jagger and Richards, the main difference was that they had learned to play and sing at home, at their own pace with no pressure, while the writing process was done under the impatient gaze of Oldham.

In the early sessions, Jagger later explained, they established the basic pattern wherein Keith tended to concentrate on the melodies while Mick wrote most of the words. Unlike Brian, however, both were open to suggestions, so some melodies would come from Jagger while Richards eventually wrote several songs, notably "Ruby Tuesday."

At first, however, Richards says, everything embarrassed him.

"For the first year, the songs were awful," he says. "Mostly we'd just give them away, wondering why anyone would want them. 'That Girl Belongs to Yesterday.' She certainly does. I know. I wrote her."

But they stayed with it. A teen chirper named Adrienne Poster recorded "Shang A Doo Lang." The late George Bean, at the time a moderately popular singer, cut "Will You Be My Lover Tonight" and "It Should Be You"—which the Stones themselves had put on tape at the "Poison Ivy" session. As heard today on bootleg tapes, the ultra-simplistic "It Should Be You" lives down to Richards' dismissal.

"Charlie would come up to us at a gig," says Richards, "and he'd say, 'I heard this song on the radio today they said you wrote. Did you really? It was awful.' And he was right. But then they started being hits. We'd look up and [see] 'That Girl Belongs to Yesterday' by Gene Pitney in the top 10."

In fact, Keith says, it wasn't until they wrote "The Last Time" in late 1964 that he began to feel the songwriting was working out. "That came right out of

At this

p o i n t

they were

closer

to

Spinal Tap

than

Lennon-

McCartney.

gospel," he says. "In fact, Mavis Staples sang it, which I loved. It was the first one of our songs we weren't ashamed to record."

Considering that by this time they had written "Tell Me," "Heart of Stone," and "Time Is On My Side" in addition to "As Tears Go By," that's not a bad starter catalog.

Still, it didn't solve Oldham's fall 1963 problem of that second single. As naturally aggressive as Easton was conservative, Oldham wanted that hit badly. He had briefly worked as a publicist for the Beatles, only to be sacked for a more experienced "pro" once his early work seemed to have paid off, and like Dick Rowe (if for different reasons), he was burning to build a rival band which could kick sand on Beatles manager Epstein's expensive trousers. Oldham had departed on friendly terms with the Beatles them-selves, however—so friendly that one theory on the problems with the Stones' mid-summer recording sessions is that Oldham was ill-advisedly trying to force a Liverpool sound out of them, heavier on vocal harmonies and lighter on the slashing guitars.

Whether that was the case or not, Oldham did have a serendipitous encounter early in September with Paul McCartney and John Lennon while he was wandering around lamenting the Stones' lack of a good original song.

Lennon and McCartney, a virtual songwriting machine by then, said they happened to have one called "I Wanna Be Your Man" which was almost fin-ished. They meant it for their own album, but sure, take it, they had plenty more.

It's tempting to suggest Lennon and McCartney saw this as a chance to place a song they might have considered second-line, a suspicion reinforced by the fact that when the Beatles finally did cut it, the vocal was given to Ringo. But Jagger was quoted at the time as saying he was flattered that they would give up such a strong tune, and in fact, the Beatles and Stones were already good friends by then.

They had met the previous April when the Beatles dropped in on a Stones show, and while the Stones were nervous about playing in front of colleagues who were already several rungs up on the rock 'n' roll ladder, the two groups went back to the Stones' place and chatted until 4 A.M. Just two weeks before the northern tour began, on September 15, they had appeared on the same bill at the Royal Albert Hall in London for a concert called "Great Pop Prom." The Stones opened the show, the Beatles closed.

"I Wanna Be Your Man" wasn't exactly in the hard, bluesy vein the Stones still professed to prefer, but the specter of success has a way of making compro-mises less painful, and Coral's pictures show a group which looks ready to get down to business. A busi-ness it was, too, because the engineers of the day were neither trained for rock 'n' roll bands nor did they care much for this one.

While some studios had been recording musical parts separately since the '50s, when Les Paul first showed how much fun it could be and the interesting effects it could produce, multitracking was not yet a routine practice and it was not about to be employed for this low-budget band. Most of the session, then, was spent running wires and experimenting with microphone placement to ensure the sound was more or less balanced.

Not that the engineers thought it mattered. But the Stones knew it did, and furthermore, they liked recording "live"—that is, with the whole band present and playing rather than recording their parts individually.

Even many years later, when the Stones had the time and money to have each note recorded separately, they would record live whenever possible, creating an amusing technological irony. The day Gus Coral was shooting their pictures, engineers who had never recorded anything like this rock 'n' roll band had no idea how to set up a studio to do it. Twenty years later, a new generation of engineers who had spent their lifetimes recording nothing but rock 'n' roll were equally perplexed when the Stones went into the studio to cut the 1986 "Dirty Work" album.

"We said we wanted to do it live and they told us nobody records live anymore," Richards recalled. "They had to figure out how to do it all over again."

With "I Wanna Be Your Man," the mikes and amps were eventually plugged in and properly arranged, and from that point on the recording went quickly. The Stones were quick studies when it came to their

▶

To the engineers at De Lane Lea Studios, the Stones were five bizarre visitors from another planet. They thought the music sounded like it came from outer space, too, which is not a wholly irrational reaction to "Stoned," an improvised track cut when the Stones needed a flip side.

music, and with the lessons of those several earlier studio sessions now under their belts, they knew what they wanted. They put a raunchy, driving edge onto Lennon and McCartney's solid pop beat and by day's end had their first good single.

"It required only an hour or two to produce their own Chicago blues interpretation of 'I Wanna Be Your Man,'" wrote Philip Norman, "replacing winsome Beatles' harmonies with the belligerent simplicity of Mick Jagger's voice and Brian Jones' slide guitar."

"Brian made that record," Richards says. "No one in England had ever played that kind of guitar on a pop record."

For a flip side, ironically, they did end up with a nominally original composition, though it owed less to traditional songwriting than to Phil Spector's policy of filling B sides with random noodling. Spector's reasoning was that first, this eliminates the possibility of disc jockeys playing the wrong side, and second, it lets the authors of this noodling piggyback on the royalties of the A side, since royalty payments are divided equally between A and B.

After "I Wanna Be Your Man" was finished, the band then sat around tossing out random thoughts and came up with "Stoned," three minutes of bluesy meandering which bears more than a passing resemblance to Booker T. and the MGs' improvisational classic "Green Onions."

"I Wanna Be Your Man" was released on November 1, a nice bit of timing insofar as the northern tour was

winding down and the Stones' career was heating up. Its immediate effect reflected the band's: Listeners tended to love it or hate it.

"The backing is wild but too prominent," wrote Pete Murray in *Melody Maker*. "It's muzzy, undisciplined and technically gives the impression of complete chaos," wrote Peter Aldersley in *Pop Weekly*, "which is a shame in these days of advanced recording techniques."

On the other side, Johnny Dean of *Beat Monthly* called it "a great double side. The Stones are rolling again."

More important than any critical assessment, the fans liked it, and it reached the British top 10, meaning it had done its job. A planned release in America was pulled at the last minute amid rumors that the potential drug implications of "Stoned" made it too controversial a risk for Decca's American label, the ultra-staid London—whose executives were probably wondering why they were being asked to step out of their nice safe classical cocoon for noise like this in the first place.

Whatever London's reasoning, "Stoned" never did come out as an American single, while "I Wanna Be Your Man" surfaced in March 1964 as the B side of "Not Fade Away."

Coral shot a hundred-plus pictures in the studio on October 7, and came away with a fascinating blend of youth and maturity: anticipation, eagerness, a look of cockiness, and a sense of possibility tempered by a

◀

While the Stones had been laying the groundwork all along for a transition from rhythm and blues to rock 'n' roll, the former was still pronounced in "I Wanna Be Your Man."

rather businesslike recognition of an unfinished task at hand. You look at their faces now, faces familiar as family after thirty years, and there's an aura about them; it's not surprising something good was about to happen. You also have to smile when you see how these dress-code rebels, the band plotting in coffee shops to overthrow houndstooth, showed up at a recording studio with jackets and thin ties knotted properly at the throat.

Ironically, Gus Coral's original mission ended in vain: Fontaine never did book the Stones for his TV show. But God blesses all photographers who do not throw away their unused work, and Coral's pictures today serve a different and more fascinating purpose: They provide some of our earliest glimpses of the Rolling Stones when success was an open question, when no one knew whether they would ever become more than a passing blip on the rock 'n' roll radar screen.

Barely past twenty, more ears, more cheeks, and less crag, Coral's Keith Richards had not yet developed the expression he wears today, the one that says sure he'll let us in on the joke, what's he got left to hide? Mick Jagger, then as now, often glances slightly away, tending to a private thought, maybe willing to let us hear half of it. Brian Jones looks one moment as if he would cross the street to avoid you and another as if he would swim the Thames for your company. As women were prone to notice, there wasn't a more innocent smile on the planet than

Brian's, nor a more effective mask for the demons that left him dead, face down in a swimming pool, less than six years later.

Complex, sometimes impossible, and often enough brilliant, these three had from the start defined the Rolling Stones. While Keith argues there would be no Rolling Stones without the drumming of Charlie Watts, and while the Stones certainly used Charlie and Bill as the foundation on which the musical house was built, it remains the musical and lyrical vision of Brian, Keith and Mick which made the Stones unique. That these seeds were planted well before the first hit record is as good an explanation as any for why they're still around today.

But these aren't simply baby pictures of some guys who grew up to be famous. They're freeze-frames from an hour of passage, from a time when the Stones knew that whether their names got into the pop music conversation depended on whether their next single would catch anyone's attention on Britain's "Top of the Pops" or maybe even, if they were lucky, American car radios. You don't have to look long at these pictures to see that they're about the music, and how intensely everyone was focused on it. Without what happened in late 1963, the tight sets at the Capitol and the second-try single at the De Lane Lea studio, there would have been no "It's All Over Now," "Satisfaction," "Beggars Banquet," or "Let It Bleed." Rock 'n' roll historians, critics, fans, and mythologists would not debate whether Mick vamped

▶

From the time Keith discovered the guitar, he just wanted to play it. Unlike some musicians, he's not an introvert. And this is his chosen tongue.

the crowd at Altamont or Keith had his blood changed in Switzerland.

It would be easy to overstate the romance of these pictures, reading into them a glamour which the reality of life on a tour of one-night stands and a slam-bang studio session do not support. But it would be hard to overstate the musical importance of what was happening at this time, the passing of a torch from Little Richard to Keith Richards, an evolution which ensured rock 'n' roll would remain the soundtrack of the Western World's next generation, with all that it represented in the 1960s, 1970s, and beyond.

This is also, in a real sense, the moment of passage in the Stones' own lives, the point at which they grew out of the skin in which they were born and matured. A reverent little blues band no longer, they were on this tour taking the irrevocable steps that would make them permanent rock 'n' rollers, in which raiment they would shock, charm, and ultimately seduce the popular music world.

Before this tour, the Stones had primarily played safe dates for audiences they knew. Before this recording session, they had only dabbled in the studio, recording a half-dozen rhythm and blues standards as well as the unlamented "Come On."

"Before," Keith told writer Stanley Booth, "there was this division between people who played in clubs and people who played the ballroom circuit. We never had to present ourselves on stage before, we'd just gone out and played where people danced. Now

we were playing for an audience that was sitting. We didn't feel we were selling out, because we were learning by going into this side of the scene."

On the Rolling Stones' side in early October 1963 were talent, passion, dreams, and a good work ethic—qualities found in, oh, maybe 500,000 other young artists. What started to take shape on this tour and in this studio was the one element that most of those other artists never find: a place to take the talent, a vision that ties it all together and puts it on the right track. Anyone tempted to underestimate the need for such a vision might remember the talented Aretha Franklin languishing without a hit record for seven years before Atlantic Records gave her "Respect."

With the Stones, there wasn't that singular a flashpoint. As far as we can tell, there was no one magic moment at which the Stones suddenly found their voice, because that voice incorporated a striking array of elements already present: Mick Jagger's unique vocals and teasing androgyny; Keith Richards' passionate love for both the rhythm and blues and country sides of rock guitar; Brian Jones' worship of Charlie Parker and pure Deep South blues combined with his restless need to explore anything new; Charlie Watts' skill at turning his rock-solid jazz drumming into economic, yet creative rock 'n' roll rhythms; and Bill Wyman's amplifier.

Actually, Wyman was a first-rate bass player and a solid, loyal soldier whose years of previous professional experience provided an invaluable grounding for the others. But it has always been a running Stones gag that he was first invited to join because he supplied electronic equipment none of the others could afford. He further played into this "utilitarian" gag by often seeming to approach the job of bassman in the Rolling Stones the way someone else might approach being a CPA at Harrod's: Punch in, do your job, punch out, go home and make precise notes on what happened that day.

In fact, Wyman was not as diffident as his latter-day reputation might suggest. In the '80s, he would spend some Stones downtime making a record called "Willie and the Poor Boys," a good-time, good-cause project on which he and some friends got to rave up on some of their favorite rock classics.

More important for the Stones story, the Wyman/Watts rhythm section has served as a prototype for much of the rock 'n' roll that followed—a fact Wyman himself may have helped the rest of the world to overlook by spending more time in his *Stone Alone* autobiography reminiscing about business details and groupies than music. He suggests the Stones were leaders in launching the groupie phenomenon, though history would suggest otherwise; perhaps more accurately, he admits they were in the right place at the right time to catch a particularly lush flowering. In any case, just to be safe, Wyman knocked five years off his age—twenty-seven down to twenty-two—so the birds would not think him too old for rock 'n' roll. Or rocking and rolling.

◀

The trick with Brian Jones, it was always said, was to get his attention and interest. In 1963, the Stones had both. They were a challenge to him, and he in turn was their most creative member.

All of which becomes relevant to this tour, and these pictures, because Wyman says this was the first point at which the groupies turned out for the Stones in measurable numbers. If before this tour the band had seriously considered whether it should stay together, as Richards and Diddley suggest, the reassuring warmth of immediate sensory feedback couldn't have hurt their resolve. Sometimes little things mean a lot.

They certainly did for the generation which grew up in postwar Britain. Americans of that era took abundance as a given; the only issue was how much of that abundance any one person could afford. In Britain, it was at least ten years after the war before preteens could walk into a candy store with only money; they needed supporting scrip because candy remained on ration. Forty years after the war, Britain still had a waiting list for private telephones.

"I think people who grew up in America during the '50s tend not to understand what it was like in Britain then," says Keith Richards. "It was very drab. The country was still just trying to put itself back together after the tremendous damage of the war. Most of our resources went into cleaning up and rebuilding, and our recovery was far slower than America's. You'd be walking down the street and turn the corner and three blocks would just be gone—rubble, nothing there. I think you have to appreciate all that when you talk about what happened in England in the '60s. The art and the music and the clothing and that

▶

Some rock bands count on their drummer to provide life on stage. Between Brian, Mick, and Keith, the Stones had no shortage of onstage life, which gave them the luxury of finding a drummer who could simply give them the perfect beat.

whole cultural explosion had been building for years."

The United States, in fact, had enjoyed a similar cultural explosion twenty years earlier. The confetti from the last VJ Day parade had barely been swept aside when America went on one of history's all-time great rolls—a nearly unprecedented confluence of optimism and supporting technology which fueled an almost tangible sense of national possibility.

To the rest of the world, the most impressive symbol of those heady postwar days was the big, bold, gaudy new American automobile. Internally, however, the more profound impact and the swiftest encroachment came in a smaller package, twelve to nineteen inches diagonal, called the television set. By the early '50s it was a standard feature of the American living room; by the mid-'50s it was the centerpiece.

But media-driven cultural evolution hardly sprang only from television. Among other things, the late '40s and '50s also saw a tremendous surge in radio stations, particularly independents which rejected national network programming to concentrate on what folks were talking about and listening to on Main Street.

Within a relatively short time, these local stations forced a fundamental shift in radio. Where the dominant stations for years had been large outlets serving a broad range of listeners over a wide geographic area, radio now became a local medium, with more

smaller stations creating most of their own programming to target narrower, more specific slices of the listener pie.

Instead of having three similar big-band or dramatic programs from the major network affiliate stations on Saturday night, the listener might now have two, three, or four times that many choices. Consequently, much more airtime became available for regional or niche musical styles, heretofore heard on only a handful of scattered outlets.

These new stations also tended to program almost exclusively pre-recorded music, which marked a significant shift at the time. Before the war and even for a decade after in some pockets, much of radio's music originated live in-studio, whether it was Glenn Miller broadcasting to the nation on Saturday night from the ballroom at the Hotel Pennsylvania or Sonny Boy Williamson blowing fifteen minutes of blues harp a day over KFFA in Helena, Arkansas.

The changeover to primarily pre-recorded music was completed only after a long, bitter battle with musicians' unions; they saw a critical source of paydays disappearing and they were right. But the live musician/radio relationship was immediately replaced with an even stronger one, in fact, one of the great symbiotic relationships of modern media: radio and record companies. Radio stations got programming free; record companies got continuous promotion of their product.

By the late 1940s, then, with radio's appetite for

◀

Like a lot of bass players, Bill was often better known for his caricature—the statue—than for his music. But he was a rock-solid bassman, combining with Charlie Watts to give the Stones the best rhythm section in rock 'n' roll.

pre-recorded music growing hourly, hundreds of independent record labels sprung up to record music which was extremely popular in specific corners of America, but which the slow-footed major record labels still treated as incidental, beneath their standards except in low-budget "specialty" lines.

Most of these new independents had pretty shallow pockets themselves, but unlike the majors, they could turn a profit with sales of a few thousand records. Happily, this led to recordings by surprisingly large numbers of Cajun fiddlers from deep in the Louisiana swamps or rhythm and blues harmony vocal groups on the streets of Brooklyn and uptown New York.

On a larger scale, it also led to widespread recording of country music (then officially marketed as "hillbilly") and blues (until the late '40s sold as "race music"). These two, not without considerable seasoning from other styles like gospel and pop harmony, became the main rivers which were later to merge into rock 'n' roll. Not surprisingly, younger generations on both sides of the Atlantic in the postwar years found the blues the more romantic of the two.

Country music dealt with many of the same issues as the blues—cheatin' gals, drunk men, hard times in a hard world—but it framed them more as specific adult dramas, the kind an eighteen-year-old often doesn't yet care about. Equally significant, country performers tended to look manufactured: white guys with plastered-down hair in rhinestone suits and great big grins.

Blues musicians, conversely, were black guys who didn't smile a lot and seemed to sing about what was happening somewhere deep in your soul. Country singers looked comfortable with life; blues singers did not. Even if blues music were not so compelling, that distinction alone would have made many teenagers feel a lot closer to the blues.

To trace the path of blues to England, to the turntables of Keith Richards, Brian Jones, and Mick Jagger, we should go back a century to the roots of modern blues performance—even though that journey dilutes some of the myth of the blues singer as the ultimate purist, the brooding artist who sings because he has to, because he is driven to express the feeling inside.

That's true to the extent that blues, like other music from Beethoven to Woody Guthrie, puts feelings into a form which can be played and sung. But even the most talented and unique of the twentieth-century blues singers, a Robert Johnson, Charlie Patton, or Muddy Waters, was only the current incarnation of a style which had been sung and passed down for dozens of generations.

"In America, what we today call the blues had been sung for many years by the slaves," says Milt Hinton, the great jazz bassist who today in his eighties teaches courses on black music history. "It was one of the styles that had come over from Africa and evolved in the fields and the cabins."

In a country where 90 percent of black persons

▶

There's sometimes a feeling that Mick was the more calculating one, and that Keith had more of a pure gut love for the music. But Keith will quickly tell you no one spends thirty years in a band without wanting it 100 percent.

were "owned," the blues provided a means to lament life without freedom, a life in which a wife could be sold away from a husband. But while the blues recorded that pain, it was also a form of entertainment, providing community pleasure when the work was done.

Then the Civil War ended and so did slavery—an essential and long-overdue moral correction which had severe short-term consequences for many of the newly freed.

"For many slaves, 'freedom' simply meant they were thrown out to fend for themselves," says Hinton. "Since it was illegal to educate slaves, most were untrained to do anything. So those who didn't have a farm to stay on would often wind up on the street of the nearest town, no money, no food. That's when they would put a hat or a cup down in front of them and sing or dance or play a musical instrument, entertaining passersby for a few pennies. They did it because that was what they knew how to do. That may have been the only way to feed their family."

It's not hard to imagine this new kind of hardscrabble life breeding more material for the dark, ominous lyrics of the blues, but most such feelings in the post–Civil War years still had to be stored away for private occasions. Challenging or even too loudly lamenting the lot of the newly "freed" Negro was a dangerous indulgence in a world where most of those Negroes still depended in some measure on the kindness of their antagonists. So most blacks learned to

smile a lot, and entertainers—whether they worked the streets, private parties, dance halls and clubs, or some combination of them all—tended to keep things publicly upbeat. Please the man who pays your fee.

Blues singer Son House told researchers in the '60s that he was astonished when he heard the first mid-1920s recordings of Charlie Patton, who cut some of the darkest, most intense, and impassioned blues records ever. House had played with Patton frequently around Mississippi, at "juke joints" and other local affairs, and he said that even when Patton played haunting blues tunes, it was never in the compact style heard on Paramount Records. In local shows, House said, Patton would clown around, play the guitar behind his head, dance, pepper the audience with off-color asides, and rarely play a whole song start to finish.

The difference in the recording studio is that the record company was paying, and the record company figured, logically enough, that flashy guitar tricks didn't sell 78-rpm records whose 75-cent price tag might represent 25 percent of a week's wages. So Patton and his fellow blues recording pioneers were told to play straight three-minute songs, preferably those which addressed what white record-company executives felt to be the true interests of the colored people: sexual double entendres, laments about bootleg whiskey and bad women.

This often condescending approach, ironically, led to some amazing music. Being forced to play his

songs straight instead of vamping for Saturday night dancers brought out some of the best in Patton, as it did a decade later with the legendary Robert Johnson.

The number of folks who saw Johnson on the Mississippi Delta "circuit" in the mid-1930s say he was just as likely to have been playing popular Tin Pan Alley standards of the day as "Terraplane Blues," and this sparks two unavoidable thoughts. First, you'd pay a million dollars to hear a tape of just one evening. Second, Johnson clearly had dimensions beyond the one nurtured and cherished by blues purists, the one where the possessed man sells his soul to the devil at the crossroads. Unless the devil threw "My Blue Heaven" into the deal.

Record companies have not infrequently distorted the history of folk-rooted music by such practices as refusing to record instruments integral to the artist, but deemed somehow unnatural by the corporation. In the '20s, the great "hillbilly" artist Charlie Poole was told by Columbia that he could not record with a piano, even though it was part of his band, because "real" hillbillies didn't use the piano. A decade later, Western swing pioneer Bob Wills had to fight for his drums.

In turn, some of these distortions became imprinted on listeners. Among them was the romantic notion that the blues evolved primarily to express the pure passion of tormented souls, when the truth is that for virtually every recorded blues singer over the last century they have also represented a pragmatic means to make a living. The Pattons, the Johnsons, and their colleagues were itinerant musicians. They'd play a juke joint one night for tips, then take a flat fee the next night to play a local society party, black or white, and wherever they went they knew the deal: Give the people what they want. A mildly naughty blues tune or two, perhaps, but mostly something they can dance to, that sends them home feeling like they had a good time.

It is from this tradition that the Rolling Stones, after an early flirtation with purism embraced most passionately by Brian Jones, emerged to become successful mass entertainers. Had they not understood the value of giving their audience a good time and the importance of reaching a wider audience, they would not have been so intent on recording a hit single in October 1963, and they would definitely not have seized upon a pop tune like "I Wanna Be Your Man."

Purity whispered, "Howlin' Wolf." Success whispered, "Lennon-McCartney."

When the Stones pulled up to the recording studio that day, Gus Coral was already waiting. He had a good view of five guys scrambling to find enough money so they could pay the cab driver. They finally got it done, after asking Coral if he could chip in, and while their dilemma hardly approached that of a slave family tossed penniless into the streets of Atlanta in 1865, it may have produced a similar determination to lift themselves above such situations in the future.

While

the band

may
have
been
named

after a

Muddy

Waters

song,

the spirit

was

Chuck

Berry.

Partly toward this end, the Stones had by now largely redefined their own original definition of "the blues." While they still called themselves a blues band and drew a substantial portion of their inspiration from the blues, by the northern tour they were meeting their audience on middle ground, somewhere between Jimmy Reed and Buddy Holly.

Practically speaking, this set them up to play for millions rather than hundreds, and while it might seem to represent significant evolution from their earlier determination to remain "pure," the band had actually never been of one mind on what "purity" meant.

Brian, at first supported by Mick, felt the blues was Muddy Waters and Howlin' Wolf—the powerhouse vocals and sinuous electric guitars out of Chicago. Keith, with Mick in agreement, heard the rock 'n' roll of Chuck Berry as the blues—tacitly arguing, perhaps, that Berry came out of jazz and blues himself and took much of what we know today as the Chuck Berry style from his mentor, the marvelous blues pianist Johnnie Johnson. The Stones' eventual emergence in public playing the music of Bo Diddley represented, in a sense, a stylistic truce, the musical middle ground.

In the end, however, Keith won. While the band may have been named after a Muddy Waters song, the spirit was Chuck Berry.

By any definition, the blues came to Britain at a leisurely pace. While the big bands with their jazz component could be heard in Britain before World War II, the arrival of more specialized styles like race (or hillbilly) music was a slow and isolated process.

World War II changed some of that, when U.S. Armed Forces Radio broadcast American music to GI's in Britain and Europe. The specially recorded V-Discs used by Armed Forces Radio, however, featured few blues singers, the V-Disc production team feeling its listeners would generally agree with their own preference for higher-class black artists like Count Basie or Lena Horne.

After the war, British listeners' selection was again left mostly to the mercy of the stuffy British Broadcasting Corporation (BBC), which had little use for the sort of music popping out all over these new radio stations in America. Whether lack of blues music was the chicken and a lack of blues fans the egg, or vice versa, the BBC held, accurately enough, that there was little demand for it.

Enough Europeans worshiped U.S. jazz artists, particularly in France, that a number of these artists moved to Europe permanently, feeling more respected there than in their homeland. But the only U.S. blues singer to have made any noticeable impact in Britain as late as 1960 was Big Bill Broonzy, who had been steadily moving away from his earlier hard blues tunes into a folksier style.

Still, cultural isolation was becoming less prevalent as communication technology expanded in the 1950s. When *Blackboard Jungle* brought rock 'n' roll

to Britain in 1955—with the predictable electrifying effect on the young and horrifying effect on their elders—determined young folks began searching for this new music and its related forms in import record shops or by overseas mail order. Port cities like Liverpool became pockets for this exotic music, brought in from New York or Chicago by commuting sailors.

By the mid-'50s, imported Elvis Presley and the homegrown, blues-rooted skiffle music of Lonnie Donegan were changing the face of Britain's popular music, just as Elvis and his cohorts were crowding aside the likes of Doris Day and Rosemary Clooney in the U.S. British fans who flipped their precious 78- and 45-rpm singles over to play the flip sides also found intriguing hints of the roots music like the blues, albeit in diluted form.

Eventually a blues "scene" developed, centered for lack of other quarters at the London apartment of an ex-Army man and blues guitarist named Alexis Korner, who according to legend got his first taste of the blues by stealing a Jimmy Yancey record. Upon leaving the service in the early '50s, Korner teamed up with fellow blues addict Cyril Davies, a harmonica player, and they made the rounds of traditional jazz and skiffle clubs, slipping blues and rhythm and blues sets into jazz performances by various bands with which they were affiliated, including Chris Barber. It was Korner's blues interlude at a late 1961 show by the Barber band in Cheltenham that introduced

▶
Because they were lugging instruments and equipment, the five Rolling Stones took a cab to the De Lane Lea recording studio on October 7, 1963. Hours later they would record their first hit record. At the moment, however, they didn't have enough money to pay the driver.

Brian Jones to the blues music for which he immediately developed an all-encompassing passion.

By the early '60s Korner and Davies had finally formed their own full-time blues band, Blues Incorporated. Their problem lay in finding a regular place to play, because all the jazz clubs were holding firm against letting this raucous noise in the door. Finally Korner talked London's Ealing Jazz Club into giving it a shot, and on March 17, 1962, Blues Incorporated opened to a half-full house of about one hundred fans. The audience included Brian Jones, who had hitchhiked down from Cheltenham, and the band included Charlie Watts.

Within a month, Korner was filling the room for every show, and just as his apartment was a crash pad for visiting musicians, the Ealing Club was their musical check-in point, with itinerant musicians invited to sit in with the band and play a number or two.

Brian sat in at Korner's second session on March 24, meeting Charlie for the first time that night, and then came back for the next several weeks as well. Swept up with the exhilaration of playing the blues to a knowledgeable and enthusiastic audience, Brian changed his stage name to Elmo Lewis, in homage to the American bottleneck guitar deity Elmo (or Elmore) James.

On April 7, Elmo Lewis played Elmore James' signature tune "Dust My Broom" to an audience which included Mick Jagger, Keith Richards, and their friend Dick Taylor. They had their own band called

◀

Okay, Bill's got a few pence. Brian, c'mon, we need a little more. No, Keith doesn't have any. Of course Keith doesn't have any. Keith never has any.

Little Boy Blue and the Blue Boys. It was their first trip to the Ealing Club and when Elmo was finished, Mick walked up and introduced himself. In the course of their subsequent conversation, Brian said he was trying to put together a blues band.

A band that played Elmore James and Jimmy Reed, then as now, would have the advantage of attracting fierce loyalists and the drawback of having a potentially limited audience and sphere of influence. The late American blues singer Willie Dixon said that when he got to Britain a year or so later, the British blues "scene" still consisted pretty much of three bands: the early Stones, who first called themselves the Rollin' Stones, the Animals, and Blues Incorporated.

Brian didn't mind. A striking figure with smooth blond hair and cool dark glasses playing slide guitar out of the Mississippi Delta by way of Chicago, he had obviously absorbed the mystique and romance of the blues. Just as obviously, he had the musical ability to play whatever he wanted.

That was immediately clear to Richards, Jagger, and Taylor, whose audition tape to Korner had just gotten them their own gig at the Ealing Club.

So meeting Brian was a bonus, and Taylor says things happened fast from there: "We were all impressed. Brian started a band and invited Mick to join to sing, and Mick said he wouldn't join until Keith came along with him. The rest of Brian's band thought Keith was too rock and rollish so they left and I joined as the bass player.

"My first impression of Brian was that he was a great musician, and with his blond hair he had a commanding image—in a quiet sort of way. He was the best musician in terms of technical ability. He knew what sound he was going for and we would rehearse every week at the Bricklayers Arms pub and later at the Wetherby Arms pub in Chelsea."

Taylor remembers things in the band being quite harmonious then, while the blues scene was slowly drawing some notice. In 1962, promoters finally risked the first British "blues" tour, though even then they hedged their bets by officially calling it "The American Folk Blues Festival." Headliners included Sonny Boy Williamson, Muddy Waters, and Otis Spann.

Tours like this are legendary among promoters for the off-stage stories they generate, many involving not-so-routine matters like finding acceptable Southern-style food for artists who tell you the least they should be able to expect is a decent meal.

Fortunately, the performers had few problems adjusting to the British audience. Not much more than a decade earlier, artists like Sonny Boy Williamson and Muddy Waters rarely saw a white face in their crowds. For some dates in the South, white faces would have been against the law, as concert venues maintained strictly segregated audiences into the '60s. But by 1962, when even raw bluesmen like Howlin' Wolf had been brought under the nonthreatening umbrella of the "folk revival," many blues

artists were making much of their living on a college/club/coffeehouse circuit where most of the faces were white. Another half decade, in fact, and many of the "blues" performers would also be white, sparking a long and sometimes bitter debate about cultural piracy from which even technical masters like Eric Clapton would not be immune.

But while many blues singers in 1962 undoubtedly suspected this new audience contained dilettantes for whom the blues was just one more transient trend, few went around trumpeting that opinion. A gig is a gig, and the folk circuit tended to pay as well or better than Chicago blues clubs.

Besides, there was always the chance some listeners would truly appreciate what they were doing, and it's a rare artist who is not flattered by a genuinely interested protégé.

A kid like Brian Jones.

"There are a lot of cats out there playing black music, but they don't understand it," says Bo Diddley. "They're just playing it. We were playing black music and Brian understood it."

Exactly how that came to happen is an important part of the story, too, and to trace the path by which blues and its frisky young cousin rhythm and blues had reached the white middle-class Britain of Brian Jones, it's valuable to look at how it first reached white middle-class America.

Start with those millions of GIs who heard some version of the blues mixed in with their Armed

▶

Charlie Watts was the quiet Stone, the stable Stone—all the things Rolling Stones weren't supposed to be. As it turned out, that wasn't a bad strategy for survival.

Forces Radio diet during the war. Then back at home, right after the war, there came a great migration of Southern blacks and whites to the new production centers of the north—Detroit, Chicago—bringing blues, country, Cajun, gospel, and other primarily Southern musical styles up Highway 51 and over the Mason-Dixon line.

This came at the precise moment when young postwar Americans, like every other generation, were hunting for a musical style of their own. The big bands and swing were for their parents, or older brothers and sisters. The new generation didn't just one morning suddenly discard the pop of Sinatra, Rosemary Clooney, and Tony Bennett, but they also wanted something with more of a beat—something they could dance to, something that felt as vibrant and alive as they did in the 1950s.

Good morning, rock 'n' roll.

This oversimplifies a decade of complex if rapid musical evolution, and it skims over important tributaries and subtle currents in the popular music river. Still, the channeling of country music, blues, rockabilly, rhythm and blues, pop, harmony quartets, and gospel into one musical form under the loose umbrella of rock 'n' roll was about as quick and clean as popular music torch-passing gets.

In a broad sense, rock 'n' roll represented a yelp of triumph from a generation which felt that, by and large, things were going its way—and, significantly, was never terribly concerned with why. Americans born after

▶

Presumable Gus Coral didn't deliberately look for an angle which would show Brian sinking out of the picture, but with hindsight this shot has an eerie air of prophecy.

1940 have no shared national crisis on the scale of a Depression or World War, and perhaps partly for this reason tend to assume that things which happened before today don't require a lot of thought or study. Late twentieth-century Americans are largely indifferent to history, in some cases distrusting the motives of those who invoke it and in other cases simply feeling impatient to get on with the present and future.

This has certainly been the case with popular culture, including rock 'n' roll. Nothing clears out a party of rock fans faster than to have someone start talking about who originally recorded all those early Elvis Presley songs, or how Muddy Waters influenced Eric Clapton.

The indifference of the masses, however, does have the salutory side effect of encouraging fierce dedication in those small pods to whom the history and roots of a musical style do seem important. This brings us back to the Rolling Stones of 1963, and Britain of the 1950s.

Unlike the U.S., the U.K. strictly controls virtually all national radio and TV broadcast outlets. The government-run BBC selects pretty much everything British residents see or hear, and not surprisingly, the BBC of the '50s was hardly inclined to turn over much airtime to this ragged new American fad called rock 'n' roll.

"Jazz and classical," says Keith Richards. "That's all I remember from the BBC in the '50s. That's what you grew up knowing."

Actually, the BBC has always been somewhat tolerant of eclectic fringes. But with a limited number of available hours and so many styles of music, few were given the exposure that could be provided even by a single local radio station in the U.S. What time did become available for rock 'n' roll, moreover, had to be split with the British version, which included cover groups, homegrown Pat Boone-style balladeers and, perhaps best of a mediocre lot, the mid-'50s skiffle bands.

Skiffle groups, the most famous of which was headed by Scotsman Lonnie Donegan, might be called early garage bands who played folk tunes on folk-style instruments. An upbeat rendition of Leadbelly's "Rock Island Line," for instance, might be pounded out on guitar, banjo, drums, homemade upright bass, and a washboard played with thimbles. Compared to Little Richard it was pretty tame, but compared to British pop crooners it was a stark-mad raveup. The young John Lennon was one of many who, in the absence of real rock role models, got his start in a skiffle band, playing all of Donegan's hits before he could tune his own guitar.

American rock arrived on the BBC first through early rockers who had reached a popularity threshold which made them impossible to ignore. Elvis Presley, Bill Haley, and Buddy Holly got regular exposure and had the same effect on some British teens as they did on some Americans: Hey, man, I gotta go get me one of them guitars.

▶

Later in the Stones' career, certain band members would develop an attraction for particular tracks and spend much studio time massaging them. In the beginning, when they cut the track live with everybody there at once, the plan had to be made ahead of time.

That was Keith Richards' reaction, and with cheap cassette tapes still twenty-five years away, he learned his early chords the same way as most of his peers: He'd scrape together or talk his parents out of enough money for a few expensive, precious, authentic 45- or 78-rpm records and play along 'til his cheap, brutal record player wore them out.

Music has been seducing people since the lyres and lutes of the ancients, and a revealing factor has always been the sociology of its seductees. The future Rolling Stones, like the future Beatles, the Who, and most other British groups, came largely from somewhere in the middle class. These were not street urchins; they had food, clothing, shelter, and families. But that still wasn't giving them the hope and optimism that had been permeating America for a decade. Their designated lot was to attend school, learn a trade, behave themselves, and grow up to provide food, clothing, and shelter for their own families. A solid goal, but not a very compelling one to a teenager, especially a teenager who doesn't think life has been very exciting and now suddenly is getting a message, distant but distinct, that somewhere out there it just might be.

A feeling like this can spread fast, and rock 'n' roll quickly became a primary bonding agent among British teens, right in there with style of dress and favorite football team. Furthermore, it developed the same sort of competitive cachet as loafers vs. boots or Chelsea vs. Arsenal.

Where American teenagers might have a good-natured debate about Elvis vs. Fabian, British teenagers—for whom access to even a modest spectrum of rock 'n' roll songs could not be taken for granted—could best their friends simply by knowing about new releases. You've got the new Elvis? Well, I've got the new Fats Domino. Yeah, well, I've got the new Gene Vincent. Thus did British teens unknowingly goad each other into a roots trip from bland white rock (Pat Boone) back to better white rock (Elvis) to black rock (Chuck Berry, Bo Diddley) to the artists they got it from (Muddy Waters, Howlin' Wolf).

"My music was received by the American kids with appreciation and enthusiasm," says Bo Diddley. "But the English kids were different. The English kids knew more about the music they were listening to. They knew more about the blues. The American kids had too much to choose from whereas the English kids didn't have that much. English promoters put together what we called 'garbage-man tours,' because the things Americans threw away, they put in their pockets, fixed it up, and sent it back to us."

And thus did seventeen-year-old Keith Richards one day in the spring of 1961, while heading for a train in Dartford, run into Mick Jagger, whom he had known briefly when they were several years younger, and rekindle the acquaintance for the primary reason that under Mick's arm were tucked copies of "The Best of Muddy Waters" and Chuck Berry's "At The Hop."

If this seems a slight basis on which to build a life-time partnership, consider that what they share through Chuck and Muddy has proven stronger than the hundreds of arguments, disagreements, snits, fights, and fallings-out they have had in more than thirty subsequent years.

Of all the things they have argued about, from drugs to women to management to what should go on the next album, they have remained linked at the heart of the music. Taylor remembers that for all Mick's grounding as a vocalist in twelve-bar blues, and for all the reverence in which he holds the blues masters, he loved to sing rock 'n' roll: "Not Fade Away," "La Bamba," "It's Gonna Work Out Fine."

Keith, perhaps because he was a guitarist, just liked anything with good chords. So he had no trouble embracing Chuck Berry right next to Muddy Waters, and he loved a good rockabilly twang, too. Before he met Mick, Keith's resumé included at least one country band, where he played Johnny Cash tunes.

The first time Mick and Keith performed together, while Mick was on summer holiday with the Richards family in the summer of 1961, they played as an Everly Brothers-style duo.

So when they met Brian at the Ealing Club, they were not as aligned as Brian with the blues purist faction. In fact, when Brian told his band he was inviting Jagger and Richards to join, they branded him a traitor for selling out the blues to these known rock 'n' roll sympathizers.

▲

Keith could often be identified by his favorite lavender shirt. He could even more often be identified by his favorite cigarette. Most of the band smoked at the time. Mick has since given it up. Keith has not.

Maybe Brian simply saw more future in working with Keith and Mick, though any potential at first was musical rather than financial, because their early gigs weren't even paying their train fare home.

In October 1962 the three decided to conserve what little money they had by renting a two-room flat at 102 Edith Grove, in London's West End. This decision was complicated somewhat by the fact Keith had no money at all, and Brian, though competent at pinching food, was deeply disinterested in holding a job. Mick kicked in some of his stipend from London School of Economics, which he was still attending by day, and pals like faithful Ian Stewart, who did have paying jobs, helped out. They still had to recruit three other roommates to meet the rent: two LSE students and Dick Hattrell, an old friend of Brian.

For Keith and Brian, moving from relatively comfortable family homes into a three-to-a-room flat made sense for only one reason beyond every teenager's desire to set his or her own rules: It enabled them to devote all their time to music. Keith held one brief job that winter, as a Christmas season postal worker, and Brian held one only long enough to be sacked for theft.

No matter. For Keith and Brian and perhaps more gradually for Mick, this was the winter when all the vague, abstract possibilities of this new music came together.

In some Stones lore, that winter has achieved a severity rivaled only by the winter Washington's

▶

Bo Diddley signs the Stones' autograph book. If they took more from Bo than his signature, he said this is one of those bands to whom he begrudges nothing. If they took some of my music, he said, they also respected it.

troops spent in Valley Forge, or the Germans in Stalingrad. But while it was record cold by British standards, and the lads rarely had enough money to properly feed the heat meter, the situation wasn't quite that desperate. Richards' mother Doris came by weekly to do their laundry; Keith went home to recuperate when he got sick; and none of their families and friends were about to let the boys starve. From the available evidence, it wasn't that much different than many young adults' first shared apartment away from home—a disaster by their parents' standards, but nothing the principals couldn't live with.

What was not exaggerated about that winter was its musical value, particularly for the unemployed Brian and Keith. "We were playing our guitars all the time, Brian and me," says Keith. "We'd play for two days straight, nonstop. Finally I'd look up and say, 'Uh, Brian, my fingers are bloody. We've been doing this for forty-eight hours.'"

These hours, days, and weeks, during which Keith and Brian practiced what Keith now calls "the ancient art of weaving," built the foundation of the Rolling Stones. Distinctive as Jagger's vocals became, solid as Charlie Watts and Bill Wyman were in the rhythm section, it was guitars that defined the early Stones records: the guitars that drove "It's All Over Now," "The Last Time," and "Tell Me" even before Richards' immortal "Satisfaction" riff dropped in from his muse one night.

So well did Brian and Keith work with each other,

so well did their musical ideas overlap and intertwine, that on many of those early records, Stones discographers cannot to this day pinpoint which passage belongs to which player. Rhythm and lead guitars blend into one. "Which means," says Keith, "we got what we wanted."

It was in the middle of the Edith Grove winter, also, that the Stones finally convinced Charlie Watts to leave Blues Incorporated and become their full-time drummer. Since Bill Wyman had already come on board, a decision Wyman recalls being certain he was daft to have made, the "original" Stones, with Stewart on piano, were in place. Their first gig was on January 14, 1963, at the Flamingo in Soho, a "cool jazz" club, and Wyman remembers the reception for the Stones as flat-out cold.

But like the Beatles to the north, the Stones had become strong enough to withstand the chill of the previous generation. They were becoming pied pipers with their own tune, already leading teenagers not into a closed jazz/blues cult, but toward a newer, wide-open style of popular music which let its audience listen, dance, or just go crazy. As the winter rolled on, the Stones got more gigs, expanded their repertoire, improved their musicianship, and started to build a reputation. They would finish their sets with an extended jam on a Bo Diddley song like "Do the Crawdaddy," and they'd have whole rooms dancing—though sometimes those rooms held hundreds of people and sometimes they still held only a dozen.

▶
Technically, Mick cannot match Pavarotti—a fact of no consequence whatsoever. He's as unique and distinctive a vocalist in rock 'n' roll as Pavarotti is in opera. And rock 'n' roll pays better.

On April 14, 1963, as Britain finally thawed out from the winter, the Stones were playing their regular gig at the Crawdaddy Club in Richmond when they saw four young fellows in leather overcoats standing off to the side. Someone had suggested to the Beatles that this show was worth catching, and apparently John, Paul, George, and Ringo agreed, because afterwards they all went to the Edith Grove flat and chatted until four about music and their futures in it. Brian got an autographed picture of the Beatles, who invited the Stones to come see their show the following week at the Royal Albert Hall.

The Beatles were a step ahead of the Stones all through this time. They recorded first, they had hits first, they invaded America first. But the Stones were doing the right things, laying down a strong musical base. What the Cavern Club and Hamburg were to the Beatles, Edith Grove was to the Rolling Stones.

When success knocked, then, the Stones were ready, and the knock came shortly after this tour ended. "I Wanna Be Your Man" made enough of an impact on the British charts to establish a radio presence for the band, and the word of mouth from the northern tour was sufficiently heady to land them a three-week British tour in January 1964 with the Ronettes, who were just coming off the huge hit "Be My Baby."

What made the world good for everyone in early 1964, of course, was the deification of the Stones' good pals the Beatles, whose conquest of America

was certified with their February 7 *Ed Sullivan Show* appearance. The Beatles not only kicked open the doors, they knocked down the entire wall through which tumbled pretty much everyone in England who owned a guitar or a drum, from the gospel-shouting Animals to the finger-popping Freddie and the Dreamers. It wasn't even necessary to be at the front of the pack to get a good shot, which is a good thing for the Rolling Stones, because they weren't.

The Stones trailed the Searchers and the Dave Clark Five, among others, and when U.S. disc jockeys were hustling to cash in on the British Invasion even as they sorted the players out, most pegged Clark's group as the Beatles' real competition. The Fab Four vs. the DC5.

This made sense from the charts, since the DC5 had seven top-20 hits in 1964. It also, however, may have represented a subconscious bit of wishful thinking. The music industry had spent a good deal of time and money between 1958 and 1963 replacing the juvenile delinquents feared to comprise much of rock 'n' roll's initial audience with a more clean-cut teenager, or at least a more clean-cut image. This made things immensely easier all around: no angry parents' groups, no payola investigations, a lot less need for damage-control publicity.

The Beatles, amusing as it sounds today, brought controversy enough—not so much in their music, which was generally considered likeable if somewhat

incessant, but in their hair, which an astonishing number of adults took as a giant upraised middle finger to all existing standards of deportment, respect, and discipline.

And these adults were not altogether wrong, so it's not hard to see how a simultaneous arrival by the Rolling Stones, a band which really did come with an attitude, could have drawn much sharper battle lines.

But for better or worse, the Stones in the winter of 1963–64 did not yet have the recorded ammunition to make any appreciable dent in the larger image of popular music. As Gus Coral's pictures suggest, they were still moving one date at a time, one record at a time, correctly realizing they needed the foothold first.

When they did cross the Atlantic with the release of "Not Fade Away" as a single in March 1964, their U.S. momentum built as their U.K. momentum had—almost subtly, if anything could be called subtle at a time when popular culture seemed to be moving at the speed of light. Where the Beatles had the top five singles in America by April 1964, the Stones didn't scratch the top 10 until later that year, when "Time Is On My Side" hit number six.

As it turned out, this methodical climb would foreshadow much of the Stones' next thirty years. For all the landmarks they carved, they never recorded the one album which sold ten million copies overnight and put them on the cover of *Time* magazine. They never had the one single—not even "Satisfaction"—

that made them the brightest flare in the sky, like the Beatles after "Sgt. Pepper" or Michael Jackson after "Thriller."

The Stones had been playing for almost ten years, time enough for the Beatles to have changed history and broken up, before the "World's Greatest rock 'n' roll Band" tag started appearing, which suggests correctly that for all its self-aware overstatement it is a title the Stones earned rather than one a publicist was able to make stick.

The Stones are more like rock 'n' roll's freight train—steady, powerful, inexorable. When Gus Coral took their pictures, they were building the engine, and it didn't pull up to number one on the U.S. charts until mid-1965—after the great "It's All Over Now," for instance, had stalled at number 26.

But by the time "Satisfaction" pulled in, Dave Clark was already settling back toward the middle of the pack, en route to an eventual career as a successful and shrewd marketer of British Invasion music. So as the Beatles continued to burn bright in the pop music sky, disc jockeys looked around for other "rivals" and this time they didn't have to guess: The Stones were there.

▶

Once the song got started, Keith and Brian practiced what Keith calls "the ancient art of weaving." Before the song started, they practiced the somewhat more mundane, but equally ancient art of tuning up.

Charlie's background was in jazz, and when he formed his own band almost three decades later, it was a big band jazz ensemble whose muse was less "Tutti Frutti" than "Flyin' Home."

The Stones got some help from the engineers in mixing "I Wanna Be Your Man," but they'd recorded just enough to know that the song's ultimate sound depended mostly on their own ability to coax what they wanted out of the studio.

▶ Since "I Wanna Be Your Man" was new to the Stones, they did some in-studio warming-up before the tape machine was turned on. In the end, though, the newness helped; the song had a freshness some of their earlier sessions lacked.

▶ After several false starts with songs that just fell flat, the group finally found their first hit single in "I Wanna Be Your Man." Richards lays the credit simply—"Brian made that record."

Keith Richards learned his early chords the same way as most of his peers. He'd scrape together enough money for a few authentic 45- or 78-rpm records and play along until his cheap, brutal record player wore them out.

Musically, there wasn't a lot to study with "I Wanna Be Your Man." But since the idea was to cut a really popular record, the Stones knew they had to find everything the song had.

▶

The Stones pretty much
had to do their own
microphone setups in the
Holborn studio, since
the engineers were as yet
unschooled in rock 'n' roll.
Here, Charlie figures out the
geography for the drums.

▶

In the beginning, Mick
had been invited to join
Brian's band. By now the
relationship had shifted, by
increments, and Mick had
become Brian's equal.
That, too, would change.

"You got
an idea

and you

couldn't
w a i t
to

play it.

That's what
it was

a b o u t

back then.

I still

feel

that way
today."

—KEITH RICHARDS

Good Golly Miss Molly

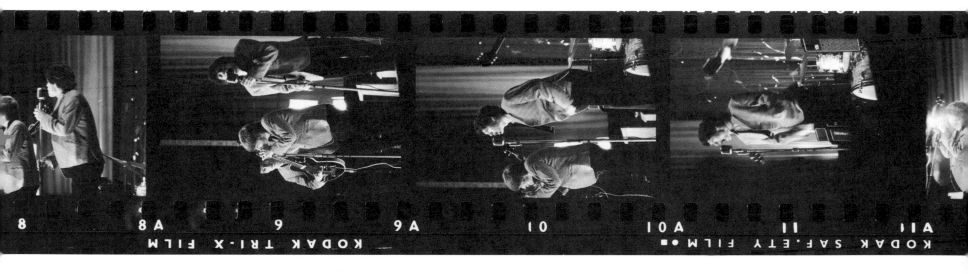

the Fab Four vs. The Rolling Uglies.

For top-40 radio purposes, this one had all the qualities any DJ could want in a manufactured showdown: friendly vs. menacing, light vs. dark, the whole nine meters. And thus were the parameters of the British Invasion forever defined in popular music mythology: the Beatles vs. the Stones.

Not that Cute Melodic Pop Guys vs. Rude-Looking Raunch Rockers told the whole story. The Beatles, it's worth remembering, were unconditionally cuddly only to teenage girls. Many parents thought their attitude downright dangerous even before John Lennon brought up the Jesus thing. Still, for publicity purposes, the Beatles could be cast easily enough as Pat Garrett to the Stones' Billy the Kid, the rock 'n' roll version of the marshall and the outlaw at fifty paces on Main Street, guitars slung low on the hip.

When the showdown came to pass, the happiest spectator was the one who had been maneuvering everyone into place for it: Stones' manager and Beatles avenger Andrew Loog Oldham, whose promotional achievements included the "Would You Want Your Daughter to Go With a Rolling Stone?" question. Oldham also made the right musical moves, resisting the efforts of Eric Easton to have the Stones replace Jagger with a "better" singer—he recognized that what Mick could sell on stage—sex—more than made up for any note he might not hit.

Whether it was designed into Oldham's hide-your-daughter campaign or just emerged as a happy side effect, what lay on the table for the Stones a year after the northern tour were far different questions than how to get two hundred Ealing Club dancers to go berserk for an extended version of "Mona." Oldham was taking the gamble of selling the Stones as personalities, a roll of the dice which can have uncomfortable consequences if at any point the public stops anticipating the music and starts waiting instead for the next tabloid scandal. But it can pay off big if the music can stay equal to or ahead of the celebrity, as it did with the Beatles for Epstein, or Elvis for Col. Tom Parker, or Frank Sinatra.

With the Stones, Oldham played just one part of the personality gamble differently: He didn't deflect insults, he encouraged them. Oldham's approach made the Stones fair game for whatever innuendo anyone wanted to deliver, and the more accusatory and appalled the response, in Oldham's mind, the more salutary the effect—which is one reason the Stones became rock 'n' roll's designated bad boys long before Jagger and Richards got around to writing "Under My Thumb" or "Sympathy for the Devil" or "Dead Flowers."

Beating Tina Turner to the idea by several years, or maybe understanding what she was already doing before she put it into words, the Stones never did anything nice and easy. As early as 1965, on their first significant American tour, Wyman recalls that they were no longer playing concerts: "We played riots and near-riots."

In retrospect, one might wonder if lads as randy as

▶

Early in the tour, the Stones played four songs a night— about twelve minutes of stage time. As the tour went on and it became clear they were a significant part of the show's appeal, they got a better program position, but not much more time. Welcome to package tours.

most of the Stones—only Charlie is said to have pretty much resisted the sirens of the road—were privately chagrined at a campaign portraying them as unwashed and uncouth. Aside from the empirical difficulty of suggesting that Brian Jones did not look as good as, say, Ringo Starr, an unattractive appearance just generally would not seem like an image any guy in his early twenties would want to carry around.

In fact, Richards says, it was not an issue. If they'd had any trouble attracting women, it might have been. But they didn't seem to.

Maybe they just needed to lose the houndstooth jackets. Whatever the reason, few bands over the years have worn their image as comfortably as the Stones, or had such a keen awareness of exactly what it does and doesn't mean, what it can and cannot do for you.

Keith Richards, arguably the best interview in the rock 'n' roll world, for years would never host one without a bottle of Wild Turkey or Rebel Yell on the table. Rare, then, was the subsequent story which did not reinforce Richards' reputation as an unreconstructed and unrepentant master of excess, with an almost otherworldly immunity to its consequences. "When I was on heroin," he would say matter-of-factly, "I still beat Mick at tennis."

If you look for Richards backstage at a Rolling Stones tour nowadays, your first good bet is to find the guy playing dominoes with his father, Bert. His most maniacal utterance is a complaint that Bert always wins.

"Anyone who knows the Stones by reputation would be amazed at what they see now," says Bernard Fowler, a vocalist on the 1989 "Steel Wheels" and 1994 "Voodoo Lounge" tours. "They hang out. You got all their kids running around. It looks like a company picnic."

If you play it right, in other words, you can keep the reputation without having to kill yourself by living the life, which by this point might wear down even the bionic Keith Richards. This is a lesson the Stones undoubtedly picked up on their own—"We learn everything the hard way in this band," laughs Richards—but it also didn't hurt that they got to spend a month with Little Richard.

By the time he joined the northern tour, "Little Richard" Penniman had built so many reputations he was like a human Chinese restaurant: Take as many as you want from any column and mix them all together. He did that himself, with some frequency. He was on drugs, he was off drugs. He was in drag, he was out of drag. He quit rock 'n' roll to serve the Lord, he returned to rock 'n' roll, he returned to the Lord. He preached, he sang, he made movies.

He was so busy defining and redefining Little Richard that he only had time in all of the '50s to cut four top-10 records, none of which rose higher than number 6 on the pop charts. One time he left the evil devil's work of rock 'n' roll so abruptly that his record company, Specialty, had to splice in a repeat chorus of his last unfinished recording so it would be long enough to release as a single. Fortunately, that was not a problem, since no Little Richard song could be harmed by adding another chorus.

Whatever went into them, they came out as the atomic bomb of rock 'n' roll. If the lyrics didn't make anyone forget Gershwin, their sheer power blasting out of a car radio speaker could turn a hardtop into a convertible. Where Chuck Berry and Bo Diddley brought a backbeat, a crackling guitar, sex, and a sense of humor into rock 'n' roll, Richard brought the gospel—a full-throttle cry straight from the revival tent that said we hold back nothing this time around.

When he converted the raunchy old barrelhouse piano chorus "Tutti frutti, good booty" into a mainstream pop hit by nudging the lyric over to "Tutti frutti, oh rootie," he drove his point home with a chorus he brought from the church and made it all sound so innocent that Pat Boone signed up for a cover version.

By conjoining the sacred and the profane, Richard was drawing on a relationship as long-standing as it has often been uneasy. Gospel was intertwining with blues or jazz even before blues pianist Georgia Tom Dorsey stopped playing "Pig Meat Strut," rearranged his name into Thomas A. Dorsey, and drew on the same musical traditions to compose "Take My Hand, Precious Lord."

But when popular early blues singers like Charlie Patton and Blind Lemon Jefferson recorded religious songs in the same guitar-and-vocal style as their sec-

What
Mick
Jagger

could sell
on stage

—sex—

more than
made up

for any

note

he

might

not

hit.

ular tunes, their record companies would issue the "sacred" songs under pseudonyms: Elder J. J. Hadley, Deacon L. J. Bates. Ostensibly this enabled devout believers to purchase music of the Lord without having their record collection defiled by the presence of sinners who were known to have recorded decidedly non-sacred tunes like "Shake It and Break It" or "Black Snake Moan."

Only trouble was, artists like Jefferson or Patton were well known for their highly distinctive voices in precisely the same communities where the record companies were selling their gospel discs. The pseudonym business, then, mostly gave everyone something to wink at.

Still, there have been and remain churchgoers who do not believe an artist can sing a gospel song sincerely if he or she is also singing about the less noble pleasures of the secular world. The late Marion Williams, who some call the greatest gospel singer of the twentieth century and who was a major influence on Little Richard, never recorded a popular song. "I like popular songs," she said. "But I don't sing them. If I did, the gospel songs would not mean the same."

Today, at fifty-nine, Little Richard says he's finally figured out how to reconcile his success in rock 'n' roll with his faith in the gospel. "Rock 'n' roll's my job," he says. "The Lord is my everything. There's no conflict with singing rock 'n' roll and serving my Lord."

If he'd reached that conclusion in 1958, he might have saved himself a lot of time shuffling back and forth between pulpits and stages. Then again, it could be argued that without the deep-down knowledge he was doing something terribly wrong and sinful, he never would have been as electrifying as he was on stage.

By the 1963 tour, that act had reached full flower. If Little Richard was at all subdued spiritually from having spent 1959–62 studying for the ministry and taking his first pulpit, none of that had hurt his ability to give a crowd a 212-degree rock 'n' roll show.

After the extended vamp that signaled his entrance, he would start at the piano, pounding out a couple of hits as he further heated the crowd. He would leap atop the piano, he would fall to his knees. Some nights he would strip, a game he knew better than he knew "Long Tall Sally," understanding that one must always keep the crowd's mind on what could come next. The band would vamp, and he would periodically check with the crowd to make sure they were still one lascivious thought ahead of him.

Today, this act might wear out in about six weeks, or however long it would take for MTV to pick it up as a video and play it to death. Thirty years ago, with no MTV, it played all over the world, especially in towns like these, and always Richard sent them home wondering if maybe, just maybe, some night he would get so caught up he would go that one step more. Even if the one extra step he really took at the end of the show was to wave his records in the air. Buy these, friends! God bless you and goodnight!

By this time, the Stones had measurable stage

▶

Hallelujah! Buy my album! God bless you all for coming to see our show tonight! We love you to death! Oooh, my soul! Good golly, Miss Molly! Buy my album!

experience of their own, and Richards says that contrary to some snippy stories—and Eric Easton's opinion—Jagger was already an exceptional stage performer.

"We'd play on these tiny little stages where he had no more than two by four feet to move around in," says Richards, "and he could do more in that space than anyone I've ever seen."

So when they got to stages like the one at the Capitol, it looked like they had a whole football field to work with. Still, no one with the Stones' curiosity or Jagger's show-business flair could have failed to recognize in Little Richard a master class in the art of working a crowd.

What we see of Little Richard in Jagger today lies more in the attitude, perhaps, than in any single routine. The other Stones have rarely shown much interest in marking time while the singer does his dance, but then, Jagger has never needed to jump astride a piano and vamp to send out sex signals. Bumping, grinding, or just pursing his ample lips, Jagger conducts a seduction his own way, with the result the same: The crowd wants a little more than he's going to give.

He didn't need Little Richard to tell him sex sells, but when Richard was demonstrating some of the ways to market it, Jagger was paying attention. That he didn't simply try to lift Richard's routines, but incorporated elements that worked for him—stressing the naughtiness he did have rather than the

prettiness he did not—provides another good explanation why the Stones have lasted thirty years.

What may also have left an impression on the Stones was Richard's off-stage demeanor, the person he became when he wasn't being Little Richard.

At all times in his life, whether serving the Lord or slippin' and slidin', Richard Penniman has had an extraordinary radar for publicity of any sort, and he is well aware that he owes virtually all the attention to the Little Richard persona. He cut several solo records in 1951 with mild success, and led the Tempo Toppers from 1953 to 1955, again with little impact. Once "Tutti Frutti" changed all that in late 1955, and the cameras fell in love with the hair and the suits and those big wide brown eyes, he knew Little Richard was a winner, and even during the years he has renounced Little Richard's music, he has fiercely protected the character.

"I am the originator, the emancipator, the quasar of rock 'n' roll!" he will proclaim to any live microphone or working pencil, and his ability to praise himself went over the top so long ago that now it's regarded as performance art, a restless and unending quest for a superlative he has not used before. This has made him a popular guest at public functions like the Rock and Roll Hall of Fame's annual induction dinner, where he can be counted on to say something rambling, amusing, and occasionally outrageous. He missed his own induction there because of an operation, so when he was called back a couple of years later to induct Otis

▶

With everyone except Charlie up front, the Stones were ready to vamp whenever an audience started to dance. Not that they could do much vamping on a tightly timed packaged tour, but it proved to be an immensely useful skill elsewhere.

Redding, he used the time to give his acceptance speech and reiterate his own qualifications.

Like Keith Richards, Little Richard gives the impression he wouldn't mind a bit if all rock 'n' roll fans assumed he lives his life in constant overdrive, spreading Little Richard everywhere he travels. One pictures him pulling into a gas station, saying "Fill it up with premium," and adding, "I am the originator, the emancipator, the quasar of rock 'n' roll!"

In truth, Little Richard takes it down several notches as soon as the cameras are off. He still punctuates conversations with reminders that he discovered everyone from James Brown to the Beatles, and his favorite metaphor is that while Chuck Berry may have built the house of rock 'n' roll, he was the architect. But ask him whether he's ever collected the money he's earned in the business, and it's clear he spends some of his time working the books. He's comfortable, he'll say. He's got enough even if it's not all he deserves. Then he'll reel off a list of other artists who can't say the same, and talk about the tragedy of unpaid back royalties. Ask him about an upcoming date and if he's not familiar with the venue, he'll come back with questions about the seating, the sound system, the stage setup. He's proud that he tends to his overseas fans, making sure to visit Germany or Japan on a regular schedule.

He knows what he's selling and how to sell it. Just as he knew it in 1963. All he can't control is time. He can't work the piano top with the same dexterity and

he has taken to wearing large amounts of makeup—so much he has to watch his distance from the TV cameras that could cause it to run. All of which makes it more fascinating to see the Coral pictures, particularly where he's simply relaxing in a chair, in front of an old window, and next to an old radiator.

Notice, first, the remarkable contours of his face. It's like wiping away all of today's makeup, all of the years, and finding underneath it a young Otis Redding, another singer from the red clay country of Georgia who looks to have been chiseled by a master sculptor from a piece of fine ebony.

Second, think for a moment how many chairs Little Richard has settled down in, the number of dressing rooms, the number of shows and supporting acts he has gone through since he left his job as a dishwasher in the Macon, Georgia, bus depot in 1951 and set out to prove, like the Rolling Stones a dozen years later, that he was going to be the one-in-a-million who made a living in the music business.

Today, more than half his life later, he's done it. Also, he understands that the time he spends on stage or in front of a camera being Little Richard is not most of his time, but if he plays that time right, it's enough.

It's likely the Rolling Stones already understood much of that principle in 1963, or at least as much as one can understand without ever having had the chance to put it in practice. Some biographers have written that the Stones were quietly disappointed to

▶

Little Richard was still commuting between the Lord and rock 'n' roll in 1963—his body in one church, his soul never completely away from the other.

find that Little Richard came to work in a business suit, but nothing about Mick Jagger's life suggests he didn't appreciate the difference between a stage persona and a private life.

Brian Jones used to half-joke that he wanted the Stones to become successful so he could work as little as possible, but back in 1963 he drove the others. Brian's problem was not an inability to get worked up about something, but disinterest in staying with it. He constantly needed to be finding something new, which he would learn quickly and then abandon—a pattern he applied equally to women and styles of music.

This obviously made him a risky candidate for a satisfactory long-term relationship with either, though his endless curiosity and exploration were of considerable benefit to the Stones in these early years. He was the musical center, pushing to make his guitar partner Keith and the others better. Once they had mastered rock 'n' roll basics, Brian's experiments with different sounds helped push the band out to the horizons of "Paint It Black" or "Beggar's Banquet."

What Brian got from Little Richard, then, was a challenge: This is where you can get to if you don't quit what you do. But the lasting message we have to think Little Richard left with the Stones, because they've played it out so well, is the message the best veterans always convey to the smartest rookies: Don't overlook the salesmanship. Once you've got the goods, learn how to sell them over the long run, year after year, good times and bad times. When a couple

page 96.

of fans walk into your dressing room, you don't have to be full-throttle Little Richard. Give 'em a couple of the right lines and they'll go back home and tell their friends, yup, we met him, he was just like we thought. But when you get out on the stage, you've got to give 'em so much Little Richard that anyone who sees you will never again settle for anything, or anyone, less.

Fond as the Stones were of Little Richard, however—Keith would later say Richard's "Good Golly Miss Molly" was the first song that gave him and Mick a mutual electric surge—Bo Diddley was the R&B pioneer whose music was most thoroughly woven into the early Stones' sound.

Falling somewhere between the pure down-home bluesmen who created the electrified Chicago blues of the late '40s and the flat-out rock 'n' roll of Chuck Berry, Diddley gave the Stones that middle ground. By filling their repertoire with Diddley's music, they were able to distance themselves from rock bands which simply reworked top-40 hits—in fact, they could maintain a moral superiority, which was important to Brian even after he wasn't calling himself Elmo Lewis any more. Yet at the same time, the Stones did not irrevocably limit their potential audience to the several hundred cult faithful who might come to an Ealing Club evening.

Bo's attraction for this young band can be seen from their first recording session, a never-issued (although bootlegged) set of six tunes recorded between January 28 and February 2, 1963, at the IBC

◀

Brian was so swept away the first time he heard a blues guitar that he began using the stage name "Elmo Lewis," after the Chicago bottleneck bluesman Elmore (Elmo) James. His first and last guitar riffs for the Stones were blues.

studios in London. These sessions were financed by the band, which had only two weeks earlier taken its final shape with the addition of Charlie Watts, and the hope was that the sessions would produce tapes which would convince a company to sign them up for a recording contract.

The songs came from their fledgling club act, and they began with "Diddley Daddy" and "Road Runner," both Diddley songs. They also recorded Diddley's "Crackin' Up," and followed this at another early 1963 session with "Mona (I Need You Baby)"—a favorite of Brian's and one of the tunes they would frequently embellish in concert, vamping as the girls danced and frenzy built.

Some years later, Richards would say that stage jamming and long instrumental improvisations, à la Cream or the art-rock bands of the '70s, were just not the Stones' style: "Long guitar solos have never interested me much, unless it's Segovia." Still, in these early days some vamping was both effective and probably irresistible, considering the effect it had on the female fans. Besides, there's no easier beat to play over and over than Bo Diddley.

When Jagger and Richards began writing their own songs in 1964, their need for vintage rock 'n' roll material diminished, but their fascination with Diddley lingered. On March 19, 1964, at the Camden Theater in London, they recorded four tracks for broadcast on the BBC, and two were Diddley tunes, "Mona" and "Cops and Robbers." (Strange historical footnote: The BBC used these tracks for a bizarre early stereophonic broadcast experiment, sending out one track over television and another over radio.)

For the northern tour, Diddley had actually asked earlier if the Stones would play as his backup band, according to Wyman. He says that six days before it started, he, Brian, and Charlie backed Diddley when he played the BBC Radio "Saturday Club" show—the first time any of the band had met him. Bo made the backup offer after the show, despite the fact that Charlie, who came out of a Charlie Parker background and was thus the Stone least schooled in rock 'n' roll, at first played the Diddley beat backwards.

The Stones declined his offer respectfully, not wanting to miss the chance to show off their own stuff and not wanting to be perceived on their first trip outside London as a backup ensemble.

From Gus Coral's pictures, it looks as if Bo's eyebrows were occasionally raised by this group of young English kids who seemed to have traces both of street attitude and pretty-boy aspirations.

"At the beginning of the tour Mick wasn't that confident in his dancing, so he learned dance steps from Bo, during breaks at the bar between the two nightly shows," says Linda Lawrence. "And his dancing improved. I remember Mick jumping into the audience with his maracas."

This suggests Mick may have been paying attention to Bo's whole band, but whatever he did or didn't pick up, the Stones were hardly the strangest

▶
Little Richard, a belated addition to the tour when attendance at the first few dates was spotty, had just joined when it reached Cardiff. Fortunately, some things are like riding a bicycle, and for Little Richard, that included rock 'n' roll and getting the attention of cameras.

thing Bo had seen in more than a decade on the road, and he says today that they got along fine:

"Brian was a real nice person. In fact, everyone in the whole damn group were nice people. Everyone in the whole damn group treated me very royally, and I've had a long binding relationship with all the Stones. I think they're great people, and I've never seen anything wrong with what they've done."

Unconditional acceptance. What more to ask from an idol?

It's also true, however, that Bo Diddley's own road, on which this tour was not markedly different from a thousand other way stations, has been marked by diplomacy. Whether it's Elvis Presley watching him in the wings at the Apollo Theater or Elton John writing songs off his beat three decades later, Diddley has seen the success other artists have built on his foundation, and he has developed a diplomatic response: "I don't care what anybody else makes as long as I get my share, too."

Much of the time, of course, he didn't. Like many other pioneers, particularly black ones, he'd be hunting for cab fare when someone else was taking his sound to town in a limo. He's spent a fair amount of time in court to get what's owed him, happily with some success, and he says most of the time he doesn't compound the injustices by feeling bitter about them. "I'm getting at least some of what I'm due," he says. "I'm making a living." Toward this end, the Stones have been among the more helpful

disciples: They invited him to play on some of their later, larger tours.

For helping teach them to dance and play, that seems like a good start on payback, and in the larger picture of music history, Bo Diddley is perhaps the most direct link between the Rolling Stones and the rougher blues of prewar America. Diddley used to listen to washboard bands in the fields and clubs. He used to listen to Memphis Minnie, traces of whose beat can be heard in Bo's. Like every single popular and folk artist, he got it from somewhere, which is precisely the reason Keith Richards makes it almost a mantra to argue that "The best thing to be said of any artist is that he passed it along."

As observations go, that one contains both romance and truth, and to music fans it's one of the many reasons Keith stands among the good guys. It has a practical corollary, however, which is that those who pass it along should also get something back for their own efforts, and it has been argued that it's easier to get romantic about the great chain of music when you are a multimillionaire than when you're scrambling to pay the rent. Modern music history contains too many stories like that of Big Joe Turner, the great blues singer who laid down one of the basic tracks for rock 'n' roll with "Shake, Rattle and Roll," yet thirty years later was dragging himself onto small stages when he could barely stand up because that was how he put food on his table and paid the doctor.

Perhaps the most important compliment the

▶

Bo Diddley was not only the Stones' idol, he was the real road warrior of this tour—the one who had logged the most miles of hard travelling, too many of them in towns where black skin meant no dinner and no vacancy.

Stones pay to Bo Diddley, then, is that they not only remember, they've done something about it.

Given the Stones' strong attraction to rhythm and blues, the blacker and funkier side of early rock 'n' roll, it would be easy to write the Everly Brothers off as a minor footnote on this tour, at least in terms of interest for the Stones. That was certainly the attitude of some of the R&B fans in the audience, who came to see Bo, Little Richard, and the Stones, then would leave before the Everlys came on to close the show. Alas, the rock 'n' roll fan will never win the entertainment industry's award for Mr. or Ms. Congeniality.

But the Stones knew the Everlys predated the cardboard-cutout rockers the music industry tried to create in the late '50s, the Fabians and Frankie Avalons. The Everlys came from the pure country music of the American South, whose roots ran centuries deep—back, in fact, to the ballads of the British Isles, brought over the water by Scots, Irishmen, and farmers of Northern England.

Country music is the other primary stream which fed into rock 'n' roll, though acknowledgment of this has never been the cool position to take. For one thing, the blues is way hipper, and for another, it has been argued that only R&B-derived rock 'n' roll is real rock 'n' roll. Little Richard, for one, holds that view: "I like country music," he says. "But rock 'n' roll is rhythm and blues with a backbeat. That's all it is."

The winner of this discussion, of course, is whoever gets to do the definitions. It can safely be said that

important elements of what we call rock 'n' roll under its broader definition flow from country music, and it is also true that when Keith Richards and Mick Jagger first sang together, it was in an Everly style. When Keith and Brian talked about breaking off into a duet act during the Edith Grove winter, their models were the Everlys. This was neither coincidence nor simply an imitation of something trendy, for the Everlys had never been especially popular in Britain.

But their presence on the northern tour did more than symbolize the way both rock 'n' roll in general and the Rolling Stones in particular drew from several streams. It gave Keith and Brian an up-close look at the interplay of guitars, and the whole band a reminder that ballads don't have to be sleepy. For all the reputation the Stones would later build on raunchy rock, they always made a point, live and on record, of mixing in melodic ballads like "Blue Turns to Grey" or "Angie." It isn't at all hard to imagine the Everlys singing "Lady Jane" or "Ruby Tuesday."

Somewhat subtler, but no less significant, early Stones recordings frequently feature harmony passages, and while Mick, Keith, and Brian do not add up to Don and Phil as a vocal package, the Stones clearly heard harmonies as a valuable element in delivering a song: "Time Is On My Side," "It's All Over Now," "Heart of Stone." Just as clearly, this part of their sound did not come from Chuck Berry or Bo Diddley.

The passing-on process in popular music does not work in such a way that we can look back and say that

◀

The Stones were already plotting to put the houndstooth jackets in their rearview mirror, but stage costumes didn't bother entertainers from Bo Diddley's school. If people are paying money to see you, the thinking goes, they want you to look better than the person sitting next to them.

on October 10 at the Gaumont Theater in Yorkshire, Brian Jones heard a particular chord from Bo Diddley, or Keith Richards a particular harmony from Phil and Don Everly, which they later inserted into the third verse of Rolling Stones song "X." Rather, the process works by absorption, and whatever the Stones had already absorbed from records could only have been intensified by hearing and seeing it performed live every night, at a time when they were just beginning to believe they could cross the bridge from Bo Diddley fan to Bo Diddley colleague. The drug of choice on this tour, in the days before the lads even needed amphetamines to stay awake, was adrenalin.

It's tempting to suggest that all of rock 'n' roll was on the same threshold as the Rolling Stones at the time Gus Coral shot their pictures, because less than six months later everything had changed more or less permanently. The Beatles gave rock 'n' roll its permanent foothold, ensuring its lasting imprint in popular culture and a billion individual lives. Their success also turned rock 'n' roll into an industry, which in many ways would make it harder in the future for young dreamers like the Rolling Stones. To an industry, young dreamers are loose ends, to be tied up quickly or discarded.

But to suggest that this imminent radical overhaul in the music business parallels a similarly radical overhaul in the music is to feed into a treacherous myth: that rock 'n' roll in the fall of 1963, halfway between Martin Luther King Jr.'s dream and John F.

Kennedy's assassination, was an embalmed animal brought back to life only by the near-divine intervention of the Beatles on *The Ed Sullivan Show*.

The idea that rock 'n' roll expired when Elvis Presley went into the army in early 1958 and was pretty much buried and gone until the Beatles showed up with shovels has been perpetuated even by those who know better, like John Lennon. It is simply wrong.

There were certainly efforts in the 1958–63 years to neutralize what was seen as rock 'n' roll's ragged, untamed fringes. These were not terribly different from the efforts in previous generations to tame jazz or swing music, however, and rock 'n' roll proved at least as resilient. Not only did it have the huge American "baby boom" generation for an audience, it had booming new media technology to deliver it and those thousands of kids who had seen Elvis on TV who were all learning to play it.

Simply put, rock 'n' roll had no Lost Years. The songs and artists of 1958–64 stand up to any other six years of rock history—including the ones that started in 1964. Artists who produced hit records from 1958 to 1964 (never mind the ones who merely produced great records) include Darlene Love, the Ronettes, and the other indelible Phil Spector artists, the Four Seasons, the Beach Boys, Gary "U.S." Bonds, Roy Orbison, the Impressions, Martha and the Vandellas, the Everlys, the Drifters, Ricky Nelson, the Shirelles, Gene Pitney, and Dion. There was Ray

▶

Aside from some of the local support acts like the Flintstones (a sax combo), the Everly Brothers were the odd duck on this R&B-tilted tour. In some venues, though not the Capitol, they paid a price for this: R&B fans would boo, throw things, leave, or do all three.

Charles' "I Can't Stop Loving You," Jan Bradley's "Mama Didn't Lie," "Louie Louie," and for sheer delicious symbolism, the best song ever written about rock 'n' roll, the Showmen's "It Will Stand."

Sure, "Johnny Angel" and "Alley Oop" were hits during those years. In 1965, "Mrs. Brown You've Got a Lovely Daughter" and "I Got You Babe" went to number one. Any era looks bad if you compare its dogs to another era's giants. Record to record, 1958–63 need not apologize.

What the 1958–63 era did not have was a dominating star, an Elvis Presley or Beatles who stood at the top defining and in a sense ordering everything below. That makes the era harder to summarize, hard enough that it's often easier simply to dismiss it and get right on to the Fab Four. In truth, however, that lack of a single dominant star provided the atmosphere in which a thousand bands, from the Rolling Stones in Edith Grove to the Young Rascals out on Long Island to the Temptations in Detroit, could find their own sound. On the top-40 charts, songs as marvelously diverse as "Little Star," "Mack the Knife," "Runaway," and "Deep Purple" went to number one, delivering the message to both fans and audience that there was no single formula. The rules were being written on the fly, and if you could catch someone's ear, you got your shot.

That the Stones understood this is clear from the songs they were playing and the style in which, judging from their earliest recording sessions, they

had chosen to play them. As they looked to the lesser-known corners of popular music for material, usually the R&B corners, a significant proportion of what they found came from 1958–63, proving that appreciating the music of those years involved nothing more complex than listening to it.

It's no accident that after they had done their studio warmups with Muddy Waters, Bo Diddley, Jimmy Reed, and Chuck Berry, they found their first great track with "You Better Move On," broadening a powerful song's appeal without compromising its message or strength.

The Coasters' "Poison Ivy," Barrett Strong's "Money" (also done by the Beatles), Marvin Gaye's "Can I Get a Witness," Irma Thomas' "Time Is On My Side," Bobby Womack's "It's All Over Now," Buster Brown's "Fannie Mae," Solomon Burke's "Cry to Me," and Larry Williams' "She Said Yeah" are just a few of the tracks the Stones found in rock's hardly-lost years. As late as 1986 they dipped back to 1963 for Bob and Earl's "Harlem Shuffle"—and made it into a top-five hit.

Looking back now with the perspective of three decades, it's simple enough to see the pieces of the Rolling Stones puzzle dropping into place. The talent, the ambition, the material, the opportunity: It was all there, catalyzed and put into gear by this seemingly routine five-week tour of the British outlands. From this distance, in fact, the harder exercise is to remember how it looked from there.

▶
A fan who wanted to see the band on this tour could more or less just wander in. And years later he could mention it to his friends and they could say to him, "Yeah, sure you did."

It was not until the middle months of 1963 that Bill, Charlie, and Ian Stewart were optimistic enough about the band that they quit their day jobs. Mick Jagger remained a student at LSE until the eve of their tour departure, and even then he secured an assurance from the school that if the band didn't work out, he could return a year later in the fall of 1964.

As they made their way through northern England, there were packed houses and maniacal screams at some shows, partial houses elsewhere. The Welsh police detail in Gus Coral's photo looks like a Monty Python joke, clearly overorganized out of concern for a potential crowd far in excess of the dozen or so women who turned up. The drizzling rain presented a tougher "protection" problem than this crowd.

Still, something clearly was motivating these women to leave their houses on a Sunday night and stand in that rain on a dreary and otherwise deserted Cardiff street. They weren't ruining their hair simply for the sport of it.

Ask them that night, though, and they would very likely have said they just wanted to see the band. Ask the band that night and they would very likely have said they just wanted to play their music.

And very soon, the sum of those answers would add up to more than any of them realized. Maybe it was the magic of Christmas. Or just the magic of music.

A rare shot of Mick Jagger in classic standup vocalist posture, with his right hand up to his ear to ensure that Brian's harmonica will not nudge him off the beat.

The Rolling Stones brought a sense of glamour and excitement to countless towns that looked like this.

At first valued for his impressive electronic equipment, Wyman quickly earned respect for his fine bass playing, and with Watts would form a rhythm section that helped lay the foundation for rock 'n' roll.

Mick Jagger sits with Eric Easton, the old-school booking agent who got the Stones on this tour. Easton didn't care much for Jagger's voice, but ambitious new manager Andrew Loog Oldham heard in it the precious and rare trait of raw sexuality.

► The Stones wanted everyone to sign the show's performance program. Brian in particular had a fondness for that sort of souvenir. When the Beatles had visited the Stones' Edith Grove flat earlier that year, Brian had them all autograph their promo picture.

► Charlie Watts signs the Capitol Theater program. Having your own publicity photo is one of the first ways your friends learn that you just might be working on a career.

▶
After the phone-booth-sized
venues on the Stones'
regular circuit, like the
Ealing Club, the stage at
Cardiff's Capitol Theater
looked to them like it had
room for the Mormon
Tabernacle Choir.

Early Stones recordings frequently feature harmony passages, and while Mick, Keith, and Brian didn't add up to Don and Phil (Everly) as a vocal package, the Stones clearly heard harmonies as a valuable element in delivering a song.

Epilogue

Of all the silly questions
famous artists

inevitably hear, one of the silliest is whether success has changed their lives. While many will insist it has not, that they retain the same qualities which defined them in their anonymous days, and while that can be true, the real answer is yes, of course, success changes things. That's the whole point of success.

If Mick Jagger remains today the same shrewd, analytic fellow who could just as easily have made a comfortable living with a London School of Economics diploma, or Keith Richards remains a sometimes-difficult man whose passion for music would have ended up shaping his life even if he had never made a nickel playing his guitar, the fact they have been the subjects of worldwide acclaim and fascination throughout their adult lives has inevitably shaped the way they lived those lives.

For starters, there's the little matter of access to more or less unlimited money. When the ultrastretch limousines pull up to the well-secured artists' entrance of the stadiums where the Rolling Stones play concerts today, the fifty-year-old men who step out no longer fumble for change in their pockets as they did back in Holborn, hoping that among them they can pool enough to pay the driver. They may have the same thing on their minds, what music they will be playing in the next few hours. But the life wrapped around that music is hardly the same.

From the dozens of books written on the Stones as a group and as individual members, what emerges is a portrait of intelligent people with a normal quota of human quirks which fame has enabled them to indulge, when they choose, at abnormal levels. The legendary drama of Keith stealing the exotic and beautiful Anita Pallenburg from Brian does not differ dramatically from any number of love triangles among friends and colleagues; it simply takes on more fascination because of the celebrity of the cast. Mick has been able to flirt at higher social levels and Keith able to buy more and better drugs than the average party-goer, but the instincts driving these behaviors are hardly unique to rock stars.

Today, thirty years after their breakout tour, the Rolling Stones have through no conscious design come to feel like friends to their fans. Keith is a father. Mick is a grandfather. They still love loud rock 'n' roll, but like many of their longtime fans they don't dance to it now with the wild, limber abandon of youth. The Rolling Stones today bring their families on the road, and fans bring their families to Rolling Stones concerts. A Stones concert crowd in the early days mostly broke down into groups of young boys and groups of young girls, hormones heated to the temperature of Mercury. Today the Stones attract a date crowd, couples coming to remember what they've always liked about rock 'n' roll.

The still-devilish Mick, the unreconstructed Keith, the stoic Charlie, and everybody's pal Ron Wood, who has now held Brian's guitar slot for three times as long as Brian held it—the band our parents didn't want us to date, or even play loud on our hi-fi, is now

▶

Keith is known as a rock 'n' roll guitarist—in some ways, a defining rock 'n' roll guitarist. But if he looks here as if he's fixing to flat-pick, that's no accident. He could pick country almost as easily as he could give you Chuck Berry.

welcome to drop in any time and remind us about the thirty years we've spent together.

At least those of us who survived the trip.

Brian Jones, the most musically gifted, schizophrenic, and self-destructive of the Rolling Stones, was beginning to fade in and out as early as 1965–66. With the Stones just reaching the peaks toward which he had in the early days driven them, the ever-shifting power mantle had by then fallen permanently on Mick and Keith, because they wrote the songs. Brian's behavior, some but not all of it traceable to drugs, had become increasingly problematic at a time when being prompt and reliable mattered far more than it did back on cold afternoons in Edith Grove. Success had placed more at stake, and Brian, who in the early days had been the band's booker, organizer, and taskmaster, now had become its loose end.

Sprinkled throughout Brian's final days with the Stones in the spring of 1969, however, are bits of brilliance—poignant glimpses of what could have been. His bold sitar lifts "Paint It Black" to another artistic level, and after the band almost torpedoed its entire career in 1967 with "Their Satanic Majesties Request," an album widely dismissed as a misguided "Sgt. Pepper" knockoff, it was the lyrical slide guitar Brian had first put on record in the "I Wanna Be Your Man" session which helped shape "Beggar's Banquet" and redirect the Stones back onto their rock 'n' roll feet.

By that time, however, Brian was effectively no

▶

While the other Stones were living at a point in which they had no particular responsibilities, Bill Wyman did. For starters, he was married. In fact, he wrote in his autobiography that that made the road all the more attractive because he didn't have to hide the groupies.

longer a functioning member of the band. Keith and Mick would put the songs and tracks together and if there was a part for Brian, they would also have it recorded by another band member or a hired gun, like slide ace Ry Cooder. If Brian made it to the studio and was intact enough to play, they would also record his rendition, then choose the better of the two.

The others simply were not going to wait, and if this sounds cold-blooded it was also wise, because most of Brian's life by now was spent either fighting drugs and depression or giving in to them; his physical and substance abuse problems rivaled Brian Wilson's. The angelic face captured by Gus Coral had puffed up, its youth cashed in at twenty-six.

Appropriately enough for the Stones, we don't even know for sure whether any of Brian's parts made it onto the final version of "Beggar's Banquet." As with many early Stones recordings, no one kept precise notes. The intertwined guitars of Edith Grove—Keith and Brian as one two-headed and four-handed musician practicing the ancient art of weaving—had become such an integral part of the band's musical foundation that discographers still debate who played which passages where.

Still, there are indications from persons involved with the "Beggar's Banquet" sessions that Brian's slide track was used at least for "No Expectations." This would be fitting, for there's hardly a lovelier, more aching piece of instrumental work in the Stones' thirty years. The song, too, downbeat and

chilling, reads all too easily as a farewell letter from the comrade without whom the Rolling Stones would not have existed.

In a real sense, the Rolling Stones chapter which began with the 1963 northern tour, the chapter that took them from nowhere to everywhere, closed with the departure of Brian Jones. The Stones carried on to rack up major hits, great records, a mind-numbing income, and an earned reputation as survivors in spite of themselves. But the Stones of the '70s, '80s, and '90s were a different band: not hungry kids out of Edith Grove, but successful professionals figuring out ways to keep their company prosperous in an industry with high turnover.

It's an enterprise for which Mick Jagger has always been suited, and the others picked up the necessary skills, though not without some stumbles along the way. When Brian died July 3, 1969, the Stones held a free memorial concert in Hyde Park for 250,000 people and then, as is their habit, moved on.

Gus Coral, the Stones' unofficial photographer for two days, also moved on. After Dick Fontaine decided he didn't need the pictures, Coral sent a few to Mick Jagger and received no reply. He filed the negatives away and went back to his camera, with which he still makes his living today.

Around 1989, his son Luke brought up the Rolling Stones photos, suggesting they should be seen. This time, when word got out, Coral says he did hear from Jagger, who offered to buy them. But as the photog-

▶

Charlie Watts looks like a post-war advertisement for the elegance of tobacco. While the rest of the band went shopping for girls, Charlie was just as likely to be shopping for clothes.

rapher, Coral felt they could speak to more than just the Stones family, which is how they came to make up this book, where they give us one more piece in a large and fascinating puzzle.

Like many famous folks, the Stones don't feel their story has always been told as they see it. But in the most important sense, they have written the main theme themselves, and that theme has been their music. Fascinated as we have been by their celebrity, it has never eclipsed their songs, and the main reason is the Rolling Stones in these pictures, the five guys who came out of the Ealing Club to play the Capitol Theater, were not doing it because they thought that thirty years later they would generate more revenue than half the countries in the United Nations.

Good carpenters do not start out thinking they will build a house about which everyone will talk forever. They want to build a house with which they, as persons knowledgeable in carpentry, are satisfied. Success is someone else liking it well enough to ask them to build another house.

Good musicians, similarly, do not start out thinking they will play music for the ages. They play music which they, as appreciators of music, find satisfying. If they play and are asked to play again, or make a record and are asked to record again, that's success. That's what happened to the Rolling Stones in the fall of 1963. They were asked to come back.

They just happened to be making themselves into a great rock 'n' roll band at a time when rock 'n' roll

5A   6   6

was about to become the Western world's dominant popular music.

Many years later, to launch the "Voodoo Lounge" tour which would bring them several hundred million dollars over its one- to two-year lifespan, the Rolling Stones took a floor at a luxury hotel in Washington, D.C., setting up a central lounge and family area for the band and their guests.

Mick Jagger, asked if with these kinds of trappings he still listens to music the way he did as a teenager, laughs and shakes his head. "I still listen, yeah," he says, "more when we're about to go on tour, I suppose, because you want to catch up then. But as much as when we were eighteen? We were maniacs then."

Keith Richards, asked the same question, says he still may stay up all night listening to blues, or jazz, which he says he's finally appreciating now after a twenty-year adverse reaction to that overdose he got from the BBC in the '50s. But what has stayed exactly the same with music over thirty-plus years, he explains, is how he feels about it.

"There's a lot of good music out there now," he says. "And if you listen, you hear more all the time, music you didn't know about before. I still don't hear anyone better than the Stones, but what I hope when I listen to bands today is that they're having as much fun as we did.

"That's what it was about back then. You got an idea and you couldn't wait to play it. I still feel that way today. I'd be doing this even if the Stones had never gotten further than a little blues band just kicking around London. I think to myself every day what a lucky bastard I am. I've never had to get a job."

About
the
authors

Gus Coral,

a freelance photographer
who lives in London, was
on assignment in 1963
when he photographed
the Rolling Stones on tour
in Cardiff, Wales,
and subsequently at a
recording session ten days
later, at De Lane Lea
Studios in London, where
the band recorded their
first hit record, "I Wanna
Be Your Man."

David Hinckley

is a pop music writer and
critic at large for the *New
York Daily News*. He saw
his first Rolling Stones
concert when their
current hit record was
"Get Off of My Cloud."

Debra Rodman,

a writer and literary agent
who lives in
Los Angeles, is the
founder of the Emerald
Literary Agency in
Beverly Hills.